AMERICAN KENNEL CLUB DOG CARE AND TRAINING

Today, as he has for thousands of years, the companion dog provides love and loyalty for people the world over. In return for all the good things dogs give us, the duty of responsible care is an easy obligation for any owner to meet. *Patrick Hatch*

AMERICAN KENNEL CLUB DOG CARE AND TRAINING

The American Kennel Club

HOWELL BOOK HOUSE

New York

COLLIER MACMILLAN CANADA

Toronto

MAXWELL MACMILLAN INTERNATIONAL

New York Oxford Singapore Sydney

Howell Book House
Macmillan Publishing Company
866 Third Avenue
New York, NY 10022

Collier Macmillan Canada, Inc.
1200 Eglinton Avenue East, Suite 200
Don Mills, Ontario M3C 3N1

Library of Congress Cataloging-in-Publication Data
American Kennel Club dog care and training / the American Kennel Club.
    p. cm.
    Includes index.
    ISBN 0-87605-405-X
    1. Dogs. 2. Dogs—Training. 3. Dogs—Diseases. I. American
Kennel Club.
SF427.A655 1991
636.7—dc20   91-8404
                                            CIP

Macmillan books are available at special discounts for bulk purchases for sales promotions, premiums, fund-raising, or educational use. For details, contact:

Special Sales Director
Macmillan Publishing Company
866 Third Avenue
New York, NY 10022

10 9 8 7

Designed by Nancy Sugihara

Printed in the United States of America

CONTENTS

ACKNOWLEDGMENTS

T HIS BOOK IS the result of the recommendation by Howell Book House that the American Kennel Club make available to the public a basic, general dog care and training book. Howell Book House has been the publisher of AKC's *Complete Dog Book* since 1972. The *Complete Dog Book,* now in its 17th edition, has been in continuous print since 1929. It is the best-selling dog book of all time with well over 1,500,000 copies in print. Some of the material in this book is derived from the health and care section of the *Complete Dog Book.*

American Kennel Club Dog Care and Training has been prepared under the editorial supervision of Seymour Weiss for Howell Book House and John Mandeville for the American Kennel Club. Three contributors must be especially cited for their work on this book. First is Elizabeth M. Bodner, DVM, who researched and wrote the book's basic text. Second is Bryan Hendrix, creator of the K.C. cartoons. Third is Stephen J. Hubbell who did the illustrations.

Elizabeth M. Bodner, DVM, practiced veterinary medicine in Connecticut and New Jersey after receiving her professional degree from Cornell University in 1988, where she also studied English and anthropology as an undergraduate. She has been associated with the American Kennel Club for over ten years, both as an editor of the American Kennel Club's official publication, the *Gazette,* and as a freelance writer. The author of the

"Healthy Dog" section of the AKC's *Complete Dog Book,* Dr. Bodner has been published widely on the subject of purebred dogs and veterinary medicine. She is currently the executive editor of the *Gazette* and lives with her family in New Jersey.

Bryan Hendrix lives in Atlanta, Georgia with his wife, Lisa, and their canine companion, Rumpus, who often serves as cartoonist's muse. Bryan studied at the School of Visual Arts in New York City and developed the K.C. comic strip while employed in the art department of AKC's monthly magazine *Pure-Bred Dogs/American Kennel Gazette.* He is now a self-employed humorous illustrator. K.C. continues to be employed at the *Gazette.*

Stephen J. Hubbell, painter and sculptor, is a native Californian. Since 1971 Steve and his family have lived in the picturesque northern California mountain community of Weaverville, where he has pursued a fine arts career in earnest. He is an American Kennel Club approved dog show judge. Steve has illustrated anatomy books on horses and has done illustrated standards on specific dog breeds. Steve is well known as a Western Artist and is a member of the prestigious American Indian and Cowboy Artists, Inc. He has had shows all across the United States and won many awards. His name is held in high esteem among art connoiseurs and his work is in collections all over the world.

INTRODUCTION

For companionship. For fun. For teaching responsibility to the kids. For pure, unadulterated love and devotion. There are many reasons, some undoubtedly more intuition than reason, for deciding to get a dog.

If you've had dogs before, but felt you could have trained, cared for or just plain understood them better, then this book is for you. Or if you're a novice and you want some solid guidance before you start raising a dog, read on.

We're the American Kennel Club, and we devote ourselves to the subject of purebred dogs. Millions of purebreds and generations of people who fancy and admire them have made our acquaintance over the last century. We know how deeply canine companionship can affect human lives.

Like most good things, however, raising dogs correctly takes effort. We're not asking you to lose your spontaneity or good sense. But if you're going to do a thorough job and avoid making common mistakes, you need to invest some time and energy in research. That's what this book is all about: helping you to pick the right breed for you and your family, maintain your dog's health and appearance, teach it good manners and set limits for its behavior. We feel this is the only way to build a healthy, longstanding relationship between you and your dog.

So, if you're ready to have your life enriched by the incomparable canine, and you're ready to assume *all* the responsibilities that go with owning man's best friend, read on.

Siberian Huskies. *Sandy Carman*

Bull Terrier. *Soren Wesseltoft*

Great Pyrenees. *John Ortiz, Jon Marie Stud*

The dog you share your life with reflects both what you expect from it and the care you devote to it. This is true for all dogs—stalwart sled dogs, playful childrens' companions, trusting puppies and many more. It may take a little extra effort to find just the right dog for you, but the results will more than justify the search.

▪ 1 ▪

BEFORE YOU GET A DOG

THE TIME HAS COME to get a dog. That's what your heart is pushing for, and your head's not far behind. Before you know it, the car keys are tight in your hand as you hasten to find the nearest batch of puppies for sale.

Before you rush off, we urge you to slow down and *think*! Getting a dog represents a commitment that may last well over a decade. It deserves careful consideration, or you may eventually wind up asking yourself where in the world your judgment was that day. Far too many dogs are abandoned because people are guilty of acting first and thinking later. We implore you not to join their ranks by getting your dog on impulse.

Therefore, we'll be looking into a number of factors over the next few pages that you should weigh carefully *before* you get a dog. This should save you, your family and your dog the heartbreak of severing a disappointing relationship in the months to come. It will also help guide you toward getting the right dog at the start.

Think WHY

Why do you want a dog? There are lots of good reasons to add a dog to your life, and just as many (or more) terrible ones.

Airedale Terrier.
Rose Richards

Tibetan Terrier.
Janet Jaramillo

So many wonderful dogs, acquired on impulse, are all too frequently discarded by owners who failed to see the long-term profile of ownership. The endearing puppy you fall in love with today will alternately break and warm your heart as it grows. Your mature companion must have the temperament to mesh with yours and fit into your lifestyle in a variety of ways. And just as dogs experience puppyhood, they cope with age. For aging dogs, a loving, patient owner is as vital as it is for a puppy. Ask yourself the right questions before you get your dog and prepare to enjoy many years of happy companionship based on the right answers.

Boxer. *Douglas T. Weir*

Remember, if you're bringing a dog into your household, it's not going to work unless *everyone* wants it to work—adults as well as kids. No matter how faithfully the kids promise, it's unrealistic to expect them to shoulder full responsibility for the puppy's needs. And remember, when it's time to pay for food, shelter and veterinary care, parents still foot the bills. Life will run a lot smoother if you want the dog as much as your kids.

Dogs deserve their popularity as pets for good reasons. They are readily adaptable. They are easily trained. Their lives are relatively long and healthy. But they are completely dependent on their owners. They must be fed a proper diet, and they need to see a vet regularly, if for no other reason than to be vaccinated against major infectious diseases. Just like us, dogs get sick—and they age, not always gracefully. When they need people most, many owners find the responsibility just too great. Please do not view dogs as disposable items, easy to cast out when the road turns bumpy. If you do, then don't get a dog. Buy something without feelings, without the capacity to return your love. We know dogs deserve better than that.

So *think* before you get a dog. Weigh all the factors carefully, select the right breed and get ready to have your life enriched by the incomparable canine.

Think SIZE

All dogs start out small. And small is rarely a problem. But what about later, when puppyhood remains only a pleasant memory? You must be ready to meet the large dog's need for large space, plenty of food and exercise, for starters. Many medium-size to large breeds are unsuitable for apartment life or any situation that limits their opportunity to work off energy. And these dogs *must* be obedience trained or else trouble is inevitable.

Where you live and how you live are important factors in considering the right size breed for you. City dwellers have different considerations than rural residents. Many apartment complexes, while permitting dogs, limit their size. This limit is frequently determined by weight. And, of course, if you're an especially finicky housekeeper, the larger the dog the larger the potential problems, even if it's just wet feet in the back hall on a rainy day.

Will you be traveling with your dog? Even a short trip with a big dog can become a crisis if you lack the appropriate vehicle to transport it or the physical strength to control it. As for vacationing with your pet, just try convincing hotel management that your 150 pound canine companion is, well, harmless. It can be tough.

Conversely, small dogs are ideal for some families but may be endangered by others. Many Toy breeds are simply too delicate to compete with a boisterous family of young children. They need to live in a protected environment, or they will not thrive.

Fortunately, it's easy to predict the adult height and weight of any purebred dog. Just find the American Kennel Club breed standard for the breed you're interested in. The breed standard

Saint Bernard puppies. *June Shew*

Puppyhood is a very short period of a dog's life. When you select a breed, be sure that the adult animal is what you really want. When you think size, think about how much dog you can comfortably fit into your available space.

Saint Bernard adult. *James Jamieson*

describes the ideal specimen of the breed. It will give you a good idea of a typical adult's size. There are separate standards for all 132 breeds recognized by AKC. Remember, since there will always be variations, it's wise to view the parents of any puppy you're considering. Size is an inherited trait. In fact, one of the best reasons to buy a purebred puppy is that you have a much better chance of knowing what it will look like when it grows up. For now, we're primarily talking about size, but several traits, from coat type to temperament, are also genetically determined.

So look beyond the enchanting puppy before you buy, and try to envision what a year's worth of growth will deliver: a perfect fit or potential problem?

Think PURPOSE

By purpose, we mean the function for which the dog was originally bred. The diversity of our canine companions is wonderful and amazing. Some breeds were meant to be hunters, others guard dogs. In some parts of the world, dogs with great endurance brought livestock or produce to market or protected the farmer's animals. Several breeds were developed to retrieve, point or flush game. Some followed a scent trail or ran down quarry. Still others found themselves pulling sleds and carts. And, of course, some breeds were developed solely to offer pleasurable companionship to their owners. Knowing the dog's original purpose can be very important in determining what type of temperament will emerge in adulthood.

Let's return for a moment to the dog whose ancestors were bred to guard his owner's flock. All muscle, with a thick protective coat, this dog may paint a striking picture. But this type of dog may not be particularly sociable with people outside its own family. In fact, it may appear downright threatening. If you are looking for a breed that welcomes every man as its friend, then life with this type of canine may prove disappointing. Someone looking for a good watch dog, on the other hand, might be thoroughly satisfied.

Golden Retriever. *Charlene Lundgren*

The functions that various breeds were developed to perform are vitally important to their suitability as companions. Sporting dogs need not necessarily be used for hunting, but they are happy in an active role and enjoy outdoor pursuits. Herding dogs, in large part, have little or no access to livestock, but they are imprinted with the instincts and perceptions common to all stock dogs.

Pembroke Welsh Corgi. *Callea Photo*

If you don't have lots of time to train a dog, you'll want to start out with a breed that has been bred to be naturally tractable. Some breeds learn commands with more ease than other breeds, and training them to respond to direction can be very gratifying. Describing some breeds as more tractable than others is not intended to be a criticism of any breed. It is a statement of fact that stems from recognizing the purposes for which different breeds were created.

The bottom line is, don't expect a dog whose ancestors have run like the wind for hundreds of generations to mature into a docile, sedentary animal. Such a breed would clearly not be the best choice for a retiree, for example, who wants a faithful, rather than fiery, companion.

So how do you avoid making this error? Go back to the breed Standard for a description of the average dog's temperament. Talk to people who already own or have owned a member of the breed. Contact the breed club for more information about the dog you're interested in. Your research will pay off.

Think CARE

The coat of a healthy dog can be eye-catching, from the glowing red jacket of an Irish Setter to the sculpted outline of a freshly groomed Poodle or Bichon Frise. A beautiful dog with a beautiful coat is a pleasure to behold.

A dog's coat can also be a dog owner's nightmare. The picturesque coats commonly seen at dog shows are hardly the result of good intentions and benign neglect. We're talking about the creation of an art form, the result of long hours of preparation before each show and even more hours of maintenance in between. In real life, given ordinary constraints on time and energy, the image would probably be quite different.

Do you have sufficient time to bathe, groom and care for the coat of a long-, fine- or thick-haired dog? Do you comprehend what might happen if you ignore this job? If drastic measures like clipping the coat to near skin level don't bother you, great. If, on the other hand, the idea of damaging a distinctive coat goes against your grain, then such is not the breed for you—

unless you're prepared to spend a lot of time using brush and comb.

Once again, check the breed Standard for a full description of the correct adult coat. See whether the breed that intrigues you has an undercoat. Many breeds grow thick undercoats that release piles of hair during ordinary shedding. Regular grooming helps contain the flood, but full-blown shedding can be horrific to the uninitiated. It can produce shell shock in a finicky

If the idea of a heavy-coated dog appeals to you, be sure you are willing to provide the necessary upkeep to maintain the dog's appearance. A dog like this Standard Poodle would quickly become unsightly and offensive if its coat were neglected for any length of time. *Gary S. Weber*

Bathing is part of grooming. Here a Newfoundland does a good job of filling the tub.   *Terry Heuermann*

homemaker, or it can mean another homeless dog. Find out about a breed's shedding characteristics and grooming needs before you bring the puppy home.

Another consideration is the likelihood of having to monitor the condition of a dog's ears. Certain breeds have long, pendulous ears or lots of hair in the ear canals. You must remove any debris and hair frequently to prevent painful ear infections.

Laziness on your part can result in agony to your dog, not to mention big vet bills. Are you prepared to assume this responsibility?

And what about eyes? Lots of dogs never suffer from eye problems as long as they live. But dogs bred to have prominent eyes need time-consuming, special care to stay healthy. Again, these breeds would prove a poor choice for the person who wants a low maintenance pet. These are just a few examples of the questions you must investigate and resolve before buying a dog.

Think TRAINING

There is little doubt that the greatest single reason dogs are given up for adoption is the failure of their owners to train them adequately. Dogs are terrific companions, but keep in mind that they are still animals. Without proper training, the cutest puppy will grow up into a terror, either unmanageable, messy in the house or both. A four-pound Pomeranian who forgets its manners on the oriental rug is enough of a problem, but when the dog is a sixty-five-pound Labrador Retriever, it's an absolute disaster. You cannot realistically live with such a dog.

Proper training means *someone* must be prepared to teach a dog what it can and cannot do. The good news is that training is relatively easy, if you are consistent and do it regularly from the day the dog arrives in your life. But you must be committed to doing a thorough and proper job of training right from the start, before you let problems get out of hand.

Think COST

Purebred dogs aren't cheap. When the years of enjoyment you will have with your dog are considered, however, the hefty purchase price should seem well spent. Even if you adopt a dog from the local shelter, there's *no such thing* as a free dog. "Free" lasts only until you get your first food and veterinary bill.

In the beginning, there are periodic health checks, vaccinations and dewormings. Your dog must start a heartworm preventative program. With a new puppy, at times you may feel like you see the veterinarian more often than your spouse.

A few months later, you should allow for the cost of neutering your dog, if it's not going to be part of a breeding program. Then, throughout the dog's life, there will be annual booster shots and visits to the veterinarian for this and that—some routine business, others due to unforeseen illness. All of these costs come out of your pocket.

Be prepared. In many parts of the country, veterinary costs are considerable.

In general, costs are lower for small dogs, since many surgical procedures as well as hospitalization are dependent upon the dog's weight (this goes for keeping your dog in a kennel, too). Medications and heartworm preventatives are also prescribed by weight, so they may be less expensive for smaller dogs. Not to mention they eat a heck of a lot less than big dogs. If price is an issue, you may want to consider this right from the start.

If you're not prepared to groom your dog, the cost of a professional groomer must also be anticipated. Some dogs require grooming several times each year—at great expense—so you may want to invest in the right equipment and learn to do it yourself, or else be prepared to pay someone else to do the job. Or better yet, consider a short-haired breed with minimal grooming requirements.

Think USE

Are you thinking about a show dog? Does home protection or perhaps a possible hunting partner spark your interest? Realistically, the overwhelming majority of dogs live their entire lives

Vizsla and Soft Coated Wheaten Terrier. *Poe Asher*

What do you plan to do with the dog you acquire? The vast majority of dogs spend their lives as pleasant household companions and no more. Pleasant companions can also make fine show dogs or satisfying field dogs. Many times, highly competitive animals spend the time between shows or trials just being dogs. You may want or need a dependable guard dog. If you do, remember that belligerent does not mean capable. A trustworthy guard dog with sound temperament does best.

Doberman Pinscher.
Barbara Eastwood.

as companions, their first and foremost role being that of a treasured pet. But if you are thinking about competing at dog shows or have any special need or use for a dog, now is the time to decide.

The sport of showing dogs has huge appeal in the United States and is pursued by tens of thousands of avid enthusiasts. A lot can be said for the pleasures of raising a champion show dog. In fact, we'll investigate this engrossing topic in more detail in chapter VI. However, not every puppy, even those with champion parents, has show potential. If you think you might enjoy getting involved in the sport of showing dogs, make every effort to explore the possibility before you decide on a puppy, because it will affect what you buy.

Furthermore, have you considered whether you want a dog (male) or bitch (female)? And have you any thoughts about breeding dogs in the future? As far as which sex to buy, remember that bitches come into season ("heat") approximately twice each year, at which time they must be carefully isolated from dogs to prevent pregnancy. The best birth control for a bitch is to have her neutered. Spaying (which makes a bitch ineligible for dog shows) has distinct health benefits, as well. We'll look into the subject of neutering in more depth in chapter III.

As for other variations between dogs and bitches (such as males being more aggressive, females more faithful, etc.), the truth is that a properly raised and trained canine makes a wonderful pet whether it is a male *or* a female.

Breeding is one activity you are best advised *not* to do. For certain, you're on the wrong track if you think breeding is a way to recoup the dog's purchase price (you won't come close, once the overall costs are tallied) or as a means of providing practical sex education for the kids.

Think SOURCE

Unless your puppy is already picked out, take a moment to think about where to purchase a well-bred, healthy dog.

An experienced breeder is your best bet for obtaining a quality animal. To begin with, breeders carefully select the parents of each litter to emphasize desirable attributes and minimize

The serious hobby breeder is the best source for your puppy. The breeder is motivated by a love of the breed and the desire to produce fine animals. Many times pet puppies come from the same litter as top winners, and the differences between them would not even be apparent to most prospective owners.

Barbara Bernard

faults in their progeny. Breeders are committed to improving breed soundness—that is, physical and mental health—with every new generation.

Another good reason to buy a puppy from a breeder is that it gives you the opportunity to interact with the puppy's dam and possibly the sire. You can, therefore, form a general impression of what the future holds for the puppy you take home.

Furthermore, buying from a breeder means that you're part of an extended family. Most breeders expect a call if the dog has a crisis at any stage in its life, so they can help you understand and cope with the problem. They seem to feel, in fact, that while their puppies must venture out into the world, they never really leave the fold. This can be especially comforting for first-time dog owners who can't even imagine what kinds of questions they'll have in the future. Come what may the conscientious breeder will be there.

Think BREED

For several important reasons, we think your new dog should be a purebred. At the top of the list are matters of predictability and reliability.

Each of the 132 breeds has been selectively engineered over time to consistently produce a dog with specific characteristics. Therefore, the purebred puppy you select today will grow up to be a typical member of its breed, with a distinct personality and appearance. This means that no surprises are lying in wait for you a year down the line; you should be rewarded with a dog that meets your expectations. Don't forget that getting a quality dog from a breeder is additional reassurance.

As for which breed to get, you alone know the needs of your family. Take your time and do a thorough investigation. To start off with, let's review the general characteristics of the breeds that make up the seven American Kennel Club Groups.

AKC classifies each purebred as either a Sporting, Hound, Working, Terrier, Toy, Non-Sporting or Herding dog. There is also a Miscellaneous class for "new" breeds; these breeds are in the process of advancing from unrecognized to fully recognized in the eyes of the American Kennel Club. The two newest breeds to be recognized, bringing the total of all breeds to 132, were the Petit Basset Griffon Vendeen and the Chinese Crested, both given full recognition in 1990. The PBGV has been assigned to the Hound Group and the Chinese Crested to the Toys.

Members of each Group share to some extent a common bond, through breeding, purpose or size. Let's look at a few generalizations about each Group that may guide you toward or drive you away from some canine contenders with no further ado.

Terriers

People familiar with this Group invariably comment on the distinctive terrier personality. These are feisty, energetic dogs whose sizes range from fairly small, as in the Norfolk, Cairn or West Highland White Terrier, to the grand Airedale Terrier.

**West Highland
White Terrier.**
Joan Snyder

Norwich Terriers.
Richard Schiller

The terriers' distinctive personality is what often endears these breeds to dog lovers. These dogs are active, self-assured and love to be wherever their favorite people are. By their nature, many terriers are diggers, and they can be vocal. Therefore, if you think you'd like a terrier, be prepared for what these dogs truly are.

Terriers typically have little tolerance for other animals, including other dogs. Their ancestors were bred to hunt and kill vermin. Many continue to project the attitude that they're always eager for a spirited argument.

Most terriers have wiry coats that require special care known as stripping in order to maintain a characteristic appearance. In general, they make engaging pets, but require owners with the determination to match their dogs' lively characters.

Working Dogs

Dogs of the Working Group were bred to perform such jobs as guarding property, pulling sleds and performing water rescues. They have been invaluable assets to man throughout the ages.

The breeds in the Working Group include some of the best-loved dogs of all time. Many still serve man in serious pursuits and demanding diversions as well.

Rottweiler. *Kathy Peters*

The Doberman Pinscher, Siberian Husky and Great Dane are included in this Group, to name just a few. Quick to learn, these intelligent, capable animals make solid companions. Their considerable dimensions and strength alone, however, make many working dogs unsuitable as pets for average families. And again, by virtue of their size alone, these dogs must be properly trained.

Akita. *Larry LaCourse*

Toy dogs such as this Pekingese were developed solely for the pleasure they bring as pets. They are wonderful when space is limited but can make admirable pets in in any setting.   *Marilyn A. Marino*

Toy Dogs

The diminutive size and winsome expressions of Toy dogs illustrate the main function of this Group: to embody sheer delight. Don't let their tiny stature fool you, though—many Toys are tough as nails. If you haven't yet experienced the barking of an angry Chihuahua, for example, well, just wait. Toy dogs will always be popular with city dwellers and people without much living space. They make ideal apartment dogs and terrific lap warmers on nippy nights.

(Incidentally, small breeds may be found in every Group, not just the Toy Group. We advise everyone to seriously consider getting a small breed, when appropriate, if for no other reason than to minimize some of the problems inherent in canines such as shedding, creating messes and cost of care. And training aside, it's still easier to control a ten-pound dog than it is one ten times that size.)

Sporting Dogs

Naturally active and alert, Sporting dogs make likeable, well-rounded companions. Members of this Group include pointers, retrievers, setters and spaniels. Remarkable for their instincts in water and woods, many of these breeds actively continue to participate in hunting and other field activities. Potential owners of Sporting dogs need to realize that most require regular, invigorating exercise.

Sporting dogs are so popular, in fact, that three of the four top-registered breeds of 1990 in the United States are members of this Group. Occupying first, second and fourth positions of total AKC registrations were the Cocker Spaniel, Labrador Retriever and Golden Retriever, respectively. Together, these three breeds accounted for nearly 250,000 of the 1,250,000 annual registrations recorded in AKC's Stud Book.

The spaniels make up just one of the families in the Sporting Group and have been known for centuries. These handsome English Springer Spaniels are typical modern representatives of this old family. *Sandra Hamilton*

Hounds

Most hounds share the common ancestral trait of being used for hunting. Some use acute scenting powers to follow a trail. Others demonstrate a phenomenal gift of stamina as they relentlessly run down quarry. Beyond this, however, generalizations about hounds are hard to come by, since the Group encompasses quite a diverse lot. There are Pharaoh Hounds, Norwegian Elkhounds, Afghans and Beagles, among others. Some hounds share the distinct ability to produce a unique sound known as baying. You'd best sample this sound before you decide to get a hound of your own to be sure it's your cup of musical tea.

Irish Wolfhound. *Janet C. Queisser*

The Hound Group includes some of the largest and smallest of breeds, as well as many of the most familiar and unusual. These dogs were developed to hunt large and small game. Divided into two categories, they hunted by sight or scent, and even today many are still used to do their breeds' work.

Beagle. *Victor Lopez*

Borzoi. *Burt Lippman*

Non-Sporting Dogs

Non-Sporting dogs are also a diverse Group. Here we see sturdy animals with as different personalities and appearances as the Chow Chow, Dalmatian, French Bulldog and Keeshond. Talk about differences in size, coat and visage! Some, like the Schipperke and Tibetan Spaniel, are uncommon sights in the average neighborhood. Others, however, like the Poodle and Lhasa Apso, have quite a large following.

Lhasa Apso.
Grace Satriale

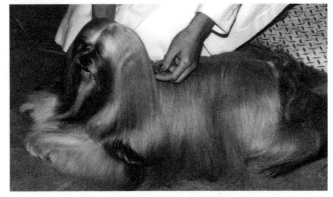

The breeds in the Non-Sporting Group are a varied collection in terms of size, coat, personality and overall appearance. Some Non-Sporting breeds are seldom encountered outside a dog show, while others are universal favorites.

Dalmatian.
Janet Ashbey

Herding Dogs

The seventh and final Group embraces the Herding dogs. The Herding Group, created in 1983, is also the newest AKC classification; its members were formerly members of the Working Group. All fourteen breeds (German Shepherd Dog, Collie and Old English Sheepdog among them) share the fabulous ability to control the movement of other animals. A remarkable example is the low-set Corgi, perhaps one foot tall at the shoulders, that can drive a herd of cows many times its size to pasture by leaping and nipping at their heels. The vast majority of Herding dogs, as household pets, never cross paths with a farm animal. Nevertheless, pure instinct prompts many of these dogs to gently herd their owners, especially the children of the family. In general, these intelligent dogs make excellent companions and respond beautifully to training exercises.

AKC Recognized Breeds

The American Kennel Club *Complete Dog Book* is the perfect place to find information on each breed. This volume contains pictures, histories and official breed Standards for all AKC recognized breeds.

Here is a complete list of the 132 breeds recognized by the AKC. The listing is by Group, with members arranged in alphabetical order. Traditionally, the Groups are assigned numerical designations of one (I) to seven (VII), with the Sporting being I, Hounds II, Working III, Terrier IV, Toy V, Non-Sporting VI, and Herding VII. You'll need this information as you go to a dog show and figure out who's being judged when and where.

The breeds in the Herding Group enabled man to change from hunter to farmer and in so doing helped advance all of civilization. The variety among the Herding breeds reflects the conditions in which they were developed and the needs of their environments. Today, Herding dogs are regarded among the most desirable and intelligent of breeds.

Old English Sheepdog.
Rebecca Sherman

Shetland Sheepdogs.
S. Price

ALL BREEDS CURRENTLY RECOGNIZED BY THE AMERICAN KENNEL CLUB

I SPORTING GROUP

Brittany
Pointer
German Shorthaired Pointer
German Wirehaired Pointer
Chesapeake Bay Retriever
Curly-Coated Retriever
Flat-Coated Retriever
Golden Retriever
Labrador Retriever
English Setter
Gordon Setter
Irish Setter
American Water Spaniel
Clumber Spaniel
Cocker Spaniel
English Cocker Spaniel
English Springer Spaniel
Field Spaniel
Irish Water Spaniel
Sussex Spaniel
Welsh Springer Spaniel
Vizslas
Weimaraner
Wirehaired Pointing Griffon

II HOUND GROUP

Afghan Hound
Basenji
Basset Hound
Beagle
Black & Tan Coonhound
Bloodhound
Borzoi
Dachshund
American Foxhound
English Foxhound
Greyhound
Harrier
Ibizan Hound
Irish Wolfhound
Norwegian Elkhound
Otterhound
Petit Basset Griffon Vendeen
Pharaoh Hound
Rhodesian Ridgeback
Saluki
Scottish Deerhound
Whippet

III WORKING GROUP

Akita
Alaskan Malamute
Bernese Mountain Dog
Boxer
Bullmastiff
Doberman Pinscher
Giant Schnauzer
Great Dane
Great Pyrenees
Komondor
Kuvasz
Mastiff
Newfoundland
Portuguese Water Dog
Rottweiler
Saint Bernard
Samoyed
Siberian Husky
Standard Schnauzer

IV TERRIER GROUP

Airedale Terrier
American Staffordshire
    Terrier
Australian Terrier
Bedlington Terrier
Border Terrier
Bull Terrier
Cairn Terrier
Dandie Dinmont Terrier
Smooth Fox Terrier
Wire Fox Terrier
Irish Terrier
Kerry Blue Terrier
Lakeland Terrier
Standard Manchester
    Terrier
Miniature Schnauzer
Norfolk Terrier
Norwich Terrier
Scottish Terrier
Sealyham Terrier
Skye Terrier
Soft Coated Wheaten
    Terrier
Staffordshire Bull Terrier
Welsh Terrier
West Highland White
    Terrier

V TOY GROUP

Affenpinscher
Brussels Griffon
Chihuahua
Chinese Crested
English Toy Spaniel
Italian Greyhound
Japanese Chin
Maltese
Toy Manchester Terrier
Miniature Pinscher
Papillon
Pekingese
Pomeranian
Toy Poodle
Pug
Shih Tzu
Silky Terrier
Yorkshire Terrier

VI NON-SPORTING GROUP

Bichon Frise
Boston Terrier
Bulldog
Chow Chow
Dalmatian
Finnish Spitz
French Bulldog
Keeshond
Lhasa Apso
Poodle
Schipperke
Tibetan Spaniel
Tibetan Terrier

VII HERDING GROUP

Australian Cattle Dog
Bearded Collie
Belgian Malinois
Belgian Sheepdog
Belgian Tervuren
Bouvier des Flandres
Briard
Collie
German Shepherd Dog
Old English Sheepdog
Pulik
Shetland Sheepdog
Cardigan Welsh Corgi
Pembroke Welsh Corgi

Everywhere you go, you can find informed, helpful dog people who can advise you on a choice of breed, direct you to an area breed club or active breeder and even help you with the dog you have. Those in the know enjoy their dogs to the full and can advise any prospective owner on numerous questions. *Jane Donahue*

· 2 ·

THOSE IN THE KNOW

It's probably apparent by now that picking the right dog is not a simple task and should not be made impulsively. The job is well worth the effort, however. Consider it an investment intended to save you, your family and the animal a lot of potential grief.

Now that your thoughts are better attuned to your individual needs and desires in a dog, it's time to contact some valuable resources and enhance your breed knowledge.

These resources include breeders, veterinarians, dog show people, friends and even neighbors. You'd be surprised by the kinds of experiences people have had with dogs over the years. Breeders, certainly, are very knowledgeable and eager to discuss the virtues of their breed with newcomers. They also offer you an excellent opportunity to see real dogs in real settings.

Don't hesitate to tell breeders what you want in a dog so they can offer an educated opinion about whether their breed is right for you. Finding breeders is as easy as looking in the classified section of newspapers or dog magazines, asking someone who already owns a dog or contacting the American Kennel Club for more information.

Also, there are numerous publications written specifically about each breed. A library or bookstore should have an entire shelf devoted to this subject. A representative of the breed club, which is organized by people who share a common interest in one breed of dog, can provide you with good references. The American Kennel Club has an up-to-date list of breed clubs and will help direct you to the nearest breed club representative.

As far as seeing the real thing, however, especially when you're comparing breeds, there's nothing like attending a dog show. Dog shows provide the opportunity to see a parade of fine specimens of each breed, and you might better appreciate whether a particular breed is right for you—or whether its tail is liable to sweep your entire collection of knickknacks off the coffee table. Seen up close, the breed that looked perfect in a photograph may suddenly make you wonder whether the kids will be walking the dog or the other way 'round.

Or perhaps you'll find exactly what you've been looking for. So try to engage people around the show ring in some conversation, since many spectators are devoted fans. Keep in mind that the ring participants are preoccupied with their work, but try to talk to handlers or owners once their time in the limelight is over. These are great ways of getting to know a breed.

Selecting the Puppy

Puppies are normally mature enough to leave their mother and littermates when they are eight weeks old. Under no circumstances should you bring home a puppy less than six weeks of

If your home features knickknacks and bric-a-brac, remember a large dog with a long tail is liable to sweep your entire collection off the coffee table.

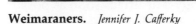

Boxers. *Janice Carlson*   **Weimaraners.** *Jennifer J. Cafferky*

Alaskan Malamutes. *Jackie Hogerty*

Even if you have never had a dog before, there are certain things you can recognize when you set out to select a puppy. A well-socialized puppy with good temperament is often a reflection of its parents. Try to observe the mother for a clue to this important aspect. The puppy you consider should give every indication of good health and vitality and should be reasonably outgoing. Also observe the puppies as they play together. This gives you a good idea of the dominant and submissive members of a litter and gives you a better chance of finding the right puppy for you.

age. It's important to know that the puppy is strong enough to be on its own.

The puppy you select should appear bright, inquisitive and alert—in other words, healthy. No matter what your heart says, do not select a puppy that seems ill or weak, or has a runny nose, watery eyes or apparent fever. The coat should not appear dull or lifeless, nor should the puppy seem thin or excessively potbellied. Also, a cowed, trembling, shy puppy or one that seems snappy and bad tempered should be avoided. Don't buy a puppy from a litter in which disease seems to be present.

It is imperative to seek a veterinarian's opinion on the puppy's health as soon as possible. Bring along any documentation provided by the seller which states dates of vaccination, parasite treatment or history of illness. Once a veterinarian has assured you that everything seems to be all right, your life with the new puppy has begun.

AKC Registration

Before we get much further, let's take a few moments to clarify the American Kennel Club's involvement in the buying or selling of dogs. In point of fact, *it does neither*. The AKC is, primarily, an organization that registers purebred dogs (hundreds of thousands annually) and supervises the sport of dogs in the United States. Nearly 10,000 different sporting events, from dog shows to Obedience and Field trials to Performance Events, are held under AKC's rules each year.

There are no individual "members" of the American Kennel Club. AKC is a "club of clubs," founded in 1884 by show-giving clubs to bring order to the sport of dogs. The second oldest sport-governing body in the United States, the AKC continues to champion the cause of purebred dogs through events that reward breed soundness and ability as well as through public education.

Your relationship with the AKC begins as you complete the purchase of your purebred puppy or dog. When you buy a dog that is represented as being eligible for registration with the American Kennel Club, you should receive an AKC application form properly filled out by the seller. Once you complete the application and submit it to the AKC with the proper fee, if all is in order, the dog will be registered and the AKC will mail out your official registration certificate.

If the dog has already been registered by the previous owner, the seller should furnish you with the dog's registration certificate. The reverse side of the certificate should be completed by the owner to indicate transfer to you.

The individual registration application, properly filled out on front and back, covering the transfer of ownership from a puppy's breeder to its new owner.

FEE $3.00
Effective
JULY 1, 1990

SUPPLEMENTAL TRANSFER STATEMENT
NOT VALID unless attached to the AKC Dog Registration Application

SEC. A MUST BE COMPLETED AND SIGNED PERSONALLY BY PERSON OR PERSONS WHO TRANSFER THE DOG.*

DO NOT WRITE IN SPACE ABOVE

I certify that on (month) _10_ (day) _31_ (year) _91_ I delivered or shipped the (breed) _Labrador Retriever_ from litter No. _SM123321/01_ DIRECTLY TO:

INVALID IF SIGNED IN BLANK

(sex) _M_ (color and markings) _BLK_

PRINT NAME(S) _MARY JONES_

ADDRESS _3 MAIN ST KIRKWOOD, MO_

I CERTIFY, BY MY SIGNATURE, THAT I AM IN GOOD STANDING WITH THE AMERICAN KENNEL CLUB.

SIGNED _Sue Smith_   SIGNED _____
FORMER OWNER – PERSON TRANSFERRING DOG   FORMER CO-OWNER (if any)

SEC. B MUST BE COMPLETED AND SIGNED PERSONALLY BY NEW OWNER (AND NEW CO-OWNER, IF ANY) NAMED IN SEC. A ABOVE, provided he still owns the dog and wants registration certificate issued in his name. If the dog has again been transferred, do not use this Sec. B, but make out Sec. A on another of these forms.

I apply to The American Kennel Club to have Registration Certificate for this dog issued in my/our name(s), and certify that I/we acquired it on the date set forth above DIRECTLY from the person(s) who Signed Sec. A above, and that I/we still own this dog. I agree to abide by the American Kennel Club rules and regulations.

New owner's personal signature _Mary Jones_   New co-owner's signature if jointly owned _____

Name _MARY JONES_   Name _____

Address _3 MAIN ST._   Address _____

City, State, Zip _KIRKWOOD, MO 64541_   City, State, Zip _____

*READ INSTRUCTIONS ON REVERSE SIDE   R 48-18 (2/91)

AMERICAN KENNEL CLUB

NAME YANKEE DOODLE DANDY

No. SM123321/01

BREED LABRADOR RETRIEVER
(108)

SEX MALE

COLOR BLACK

DATE OF BIRTH JULY 13 1991

SIRE FLD CH BLACK BART SE654321 (6–86)

DAM SUSIE CUE SM069393/02 (11–91)

BREEDER JOHN Q PUBLIC

IF A DATE APPEARS AFTER THE NAME AND NUMBER OF THE SIRE AND DAM, IT INDICATES THE ISSUE OF THE STUD BOOK REGISTER IN WHICH THE SIRE OR DAM IS PUBLISHED.

OWNER MARY JONES
3 MAIN STREET
KIRKWOOD, MO 64541

CERTIFICATE ISSUED DEC 1 1991

THIS CERTIFICATE ISSUED WITH THE RIGHT TO CORRECT OR REVOKE BY THE AMERICAN KENNEL CLUB

See Transfer Instructions on Back of Certificate

REGISTRATION CERTIFICATE

If, prior to registering the puppy in her own name, the new owner decides she doesn't want the puppy and transfers it to another person, a supplemental transfer statement must be completed and sent along with the original application. If the person who acquires the dog sends in these two forms to the American Kennel Club, along with the required fee, an individual registration certificate will be made out and issued in the name of the new owner.

If the seller does not have the AKC registration application or registration certificate available at the time you acquire the dog, the seller should give you a written bill of sale that includes the following information:

- breed, sex and color of the dog
- date of birth of the dog
- registered names and numbers of the dog's sire and dam
- name and address of the breeder.

The bill of sale should also indicate when you may expect to receive the actual AKC registration papers. Anyone acquiring a dog represented as being eligible for AKC registration should realize that it is their responsibility to obtain complete identification of the dog as described above. If the seller is unable or unwilling to provide either proper AKC papers or a signed bill of sale with complete identifying information, *do not buy the dog*.

If you have complete breeding information but are experiencing difficulty obtaining registration papers, contact the AKC. Send along copies of your bill of sale or the identifying information you received at the time of purchase, the complete name and address of the person from whom you acquired the dog and an explanation of what efforts you have made to obtain the papers. Send the information to the American Kennel Club, 5580 Centerview Drive, Raleigh, NC 27606.

Limited Registration

The AKC also provides breeders with a limited registration option. This option permits breeders to register dogs as "not for breeding purposes." This means that in the opinion of the breeder, the puppy demonstrates a trait that he or she does not wish to perpetuate. This is for the good of the breed. For example, it might be something undesirable about the animal's markings or the way it holds its tail.

Dogs with limited registration are likely to otherwise make outstanding pets; it's not as if you're taking home a defective animal. Also, the asking price for the limited registration puppy will probably be considerably less than for a littermate of higher quality. This might be a good choice for you.

"AKC Reg." Kennels—What Does it Mean?

Many people want to know the significance of "AKC Reg." when it appears after the name of a kennel. This simply means that the kennel's name is protected for the sole use of its owner in *naming* dogs to be registered. It does not imply any special stamp of approval by AKC.

The American Kennel Club and Quality

The serious breeders and exhibitors who founded the American Kennel Club as an organization to protect and promote pure-bred dogs have been successful beyond their wildest dreams. Not only have purebred dogs emerged as the beloved companions of many millions of Americans, but also the very identification of dogs as "AKC registered" has become synonymous with "quality" in the eyes of the public.

This has come about for good reason. The serious dog fancy in this country has bred outstanding dogs, dogs with stable temperaments and healthy bodies—and good looks to boot. Today's dogs are the result of untold years of devoted work by breeders to concentrate the best in their breed. They've carefully scrutinized each sire and dam before using them to perpetuate their kind, and then provided mother and offspring with the absolute best care possible for a good start in life.

On September 18, 1984, the American Kennel Club marked its 100th anniversary of continued operation as the primary registering body for purebred dogs in the United States. Many involved in the dog fancy took special note of the AKC Centennial. Even K.C. took time to call and find out if there was anything he could do. AKC's response was obvious.

Take advantage of the sweat and tears breeders pour into their work and buy a quality puppy for your family. They're not difficult to find. If you think that buying puppies from breeders means dealing with conceited snobs, you're in for a surprise. You're also going to be surprised if you think that the price of a pet puppy from a serious breeder will always be too high. Actually, you can expect to pay no more, and in many cases considerably less, for a puppy from a serious breeder as opposed to one from a typical retail source of supply.

So, please think long and hard about getting a dog. Then think again. The effort you put into deciding what breed is right for you and then obtaining the dog from the best possible source will reward you many times over during the dog's lifetime.

While being separated from mother and siblings is traumatic for many puppies, they soon learn that they don't need to share their new people with any other dogs. Best of all, the adjustment period is usually very brief. This Pembroke Welsh Corgi puppy is losing no time making new friends. *Jan Kirkwood*

·3·

GETTING STARTED

Not surprisingly, your new puppy may seem a little lonely for the first few days. Try looking at circumstances from its point of view: one moment it's hanging around with its mother, brothers and sisters, romping and napping and feeling secure in the crowd. Suddenly, the scene is absolutely unfamiliar, and it's all *alone*. Who wouldn't be a little shaken up?

But then your puppy will start to recognize *you* as "family" and learn that your home is its source of comfort and happiness. The bond between you will begin to form and grow before you know it. So hang in there for the first few nights when you hear signs of distress and lend support from the heart, which is easy, and the head, which may require some adjustment on your part.

Housebreaking Your Dog

Dogs are not good companions unless they are completely housebroken—no "accidents," not even an occasional one. Otherwise, you can't trust them inside your home for fear they'll do the unthinkable, and repeated episodes of this kind will surely strain your relationship.

In fact, armies of dogs are abandoned each year by people who claim their dogs are incapable of being housebroken. This is a fallacy. All dogs can be housebroken, if their owners are consistent as well as persistent in training them. Some breeds need more time to learn the lesson than other breeds, but no normal dog is a hopeless case.

Be fair. Don't expect a puppy to train itself and don't expect total control overnight. Just select a method of housebreaking and follow it to the letter until the job is done. There will be training lapses in the beginning, probably just about when you think you're home free. This is only natural and just means that you'll have to retreat a little and refresh the dog's memory. Once the message is instilled, however, it should take the most extreme of circumstances (like being ill) to make your dog violate its training.

There are two basic housebreaking techniques: crate training and paper training. Crate training is preferred, because it teaches direct housebreaking; that is, the single appropriate place to be used for elimination is the great outdoors. Paper training, unless you want your dog to continue eliminating in a designated location inside your home, should be viewed as an intermediate step toward teaching control, until the dog is taken out. You may need to employ paper training because of treacherous weather conditions or because you've been advised not to expose the puppy to the outdoors until its inoculations have given it adequate immunity against disease. On the other hand, some apartment dwellers with small dogs are content to live with a paper-trained animal on a permanent basis for the sake of convenience.

Paper Training

To paper train a dog, cover the entire floor of a room or confined space with several thicknesses of newspaper and restrict the puppy to that area. Wait for it to use the papers, then pick up the soiled sheets and replace them. Continue in this fashion for a day or two. Then leave a small corner of the room bare, and hope the dog doesn't use this. If it does, chastise it mildly and put it on the papers, letting it know that is the one and only place for it to go.

As soon as the dog seems to understand the paper concept, widen the bare area until you have left a papered space equivalent to about two full newspaper sheets. Allow your dog to use that area until it is ready to go outdoors. Then begin walking with it until it learns that the street is the proper place for

Bullmastiffs. *Dietrich*

Puppies that have been raised on newspaper often paper-train themselves. With very large breeds, however, the sooner a puppy becomes trained outdoors, the better. Today, many puppies are house-broken with the use of a crate. This is both natural and desirable; a dog will almost never soil its own "den."

Sussex Spaniel. *Kim Williams*

elimination, then remove the papers. At that point, carefully observe the dog for indications that it needs to go out (it may search frantically for the papers) and walk it immediately. Until the housebreaking idea is firmly understood, keep the puppy absolutely confined to the paper-training area.

Crate Training

Crate training is simple. Basically, it involves taking the puppy outside frequently, where it's praised for relieving itself. When the puppy's inside, it's either confined to a large sleeping-living box (the crate) or has carefully supervised liberty. At night or when you're about to leave for a few hours, the puppy is taken outside, and then placed in its crate. When you get up in the morning or arrive home, the puppy is immediately taken outside again and then given freedom to play in a confined area under your watchful eye.

Some experts in animal behavior think that puppies adapt readily to crate training because their wild ancestors were den animals, and the crate becomes your puppy's personal den. Training then proceeds on the simple principle that dogs, as naturally clean animals, will do what they can to avoid soiling their den space. Therefore, by confining a puppy to its crate at certain times of the day and night, it learns to control the urge to empty its bladder or bowels until it's allowed outside, whereupon it is rewarded through praise for a job well done.

If errors happen, and they will from time to time during the training period, chastise the puppy mildly and immediately take it outside to an area it has used previously, to remind it about the only permissible place to go. Remember to be fair, however. A young puppy needs to eliminate often, so take it out as often as you can in the early days before it has developed a measure of control. Puppies must be taken out about an hour after each feeding. Gradually, with age, your puppy will be able to contain itself for longer periods, and you can reduce the required outings to approximately four daily.

A crate is nothing more than a sturdy enclosure, which you can buy or build, similar in shape to the containers used by airlines for animal transport. Try not to think about this process

Provided your puppy is old enough to stay clean overnight, if it is let out of its crate into the yard or walked on a lead immediately upon being let out of the crate it will soon learn, as have these German Shepherd youngsters, where the right place is. *Catherine H. Brown*

as putting the puppy in a cage, with all of its negative connotations. It is *not* a jail cell or an instrument of punishment. In fact, many people find that puppies soon regard the crate as a place to retreat whenever they feel like having peace and quiet. They actually seem to appreciate possessing private space. Having a dog accustomed to being crated is also practical when you're traveling, because it controls the animal's movement and offers restraint and protection if something unplanned happens.

Many people buy a crate from a pet shop. Making your own crate, however, should not be difficult. Just be sure to build one that is strong, with secure footing and good ventilation. Ask your puppy's breeder if he or she has a spare crate or can tell you where to get one. You should aim for a clean, well-constructed enclosure with enough space for the puppy to rest comfortably, stand and turn around.

If the puppy persists in using the crate as an outhouse, your problem may be excessive space. In that case, the puppy believes his sleeping requirements are well met on one end, so it might as well use the other end to relieve itself. You may be able to solve the problem by making a simple partition for the crate interior, progressively moving it back as the puppy grows.

And lastly, never, ever leave an untrained puppy in a situation where it can get into trouble or cause damage. When you open the door of the crate the dog must always be under close supervision. Will a young, teething puppy chew on your furniture? There's a good chance it will do just that, if you turn your back. So don't offer the opportunity. Make sure you have a safe place to leave your puppy whenever it can't be watched. We're making this point as emphatically as possible so that you don't become disenchanted by misbehavior you could easily have prevented.

Feeding

Here's another good reason to seek a puppy from a reputable breeder: you'll probably go home not only with a healthy dog, but also with a detailed description of diet, a temporary supply of food and feeding instructions. If this information hasn't been offered, ask. It eases the puppy's transition to the new environ-

Welsh Terrier. *Bardi McLennan*

As with socialization, a sincere breeder makes sure puppies are fed the right food in the proper amounts. Well-fed youngsters will also reflect this fact about themselves.

Norwegian Elkhounds. *Beresford*

ment and helps prevent the gastric upset that may accompany an abrupt change of diet.

All puppies should be fed a diet designed for young, growing dogs (otherwise known simply as puppy food). Adult dog food is inappropriate at this phase of life, when puppies have special nutritional requirements for normal development. Feeding adult food will only rob your puppy of important nutrients, and the animal may not reach its full potential. Most name-brand puppy foods meet or exceed the recommendations of the National Research Council (NRC) for growth; look for this assurance on the dog food label. Whichever brand you use, stay away from generic label dog foods. Even though the lower price is attractive, the ingredients in these foods may not be in a form that is useful to the puppy. Stay with reputable name-brand dog food companies. In the pet food world, you get what you pay for.

How much and how often to feed your puppy depends on its size and weight, as well as on other factors. Three feedings a day are usually adequate to meet nutritional demands. Hold to this schedule until the puppy is four to six months old and its stomach can accommodate larger amounts of food. Then you can cut back to two meals a day. Most dogs are fed once daily when they reach one year of age.

It is very important to prevent your puppy from becoming overweight, since obesity can lead to all sorts of health problems. Fat dogs are far too common. Try not to feed any table scraps and keep the amount of treats to an absolute minimum. These are often the greatest source of unneeded calories. Weigh the puppy weekly and record its development, comparing it with published charts for the breed. You can then adjust the amount of food it's getting to conform with that for an average rate of growth. Plenty of exercise is important at this time, but make sure the puppy exercises on surfaces that are not too slippery or hard or else it may injure itself.

(A quick note: weighing a dog, even a puppy who won't sit still, is easy. Just weigh yourself, then weigh yourself holding the puppy, and deduct the difference—that's the puppy.)

Try not to be too worried if your puppy skips a meal or picks at food occasionally. It could mean that it's ready to eliminate a feeding or the quantity of food can be reduced. Most dogs finish their meals quickly, although this is not always the case. If you want to discourage the development of picky habits, try to feed at regular times in regular amounts, and don't leave food down longer than ten to twenty minutes. Fresh water, in a clean bowl, should be available at all times.

Types of Food

Manufactured dog food is widely available in three types: canned (moist), semimoist and dry (kibble). You may also be able to obtain frozen dog food in your area.

Canned food is the most expensive to feed and is often found most palatable by dogs. Be careful of "all meat" claims. Your dog should have a complete, balanced diet to fulfill all the nutritional needs, and meat alone won't do it. Check the label to see that the food meets or exceeds NRC requirements.

Semimoist foods are available in one-serving packets; usually the food is manufactured to look like chopped meat in one form or another. Name-brand semimoist foods provide a complete diet.

Dry or kibble/biscuit dog foods are the most economical. Name brands offer a complete and balanced diet, providing everything your dog needs for its particular life-style. Dry food can be fed exactly as it comes from the bag. The good thing about feeding kibble dry is that it can be removed and used later if the dog does not finish a serving. Kibble can be moistened, either with water (some brands claim a "gravy" is released on moistening) or canned food or other supplement. Although unnecessary, such supplementation may make the food more palatable to your dog.

Special foods are also commercially available for older dogs, overweight dogs and dogs undergoing exceptional stress (lactating bitches, hunting dogs and so on). When medically necessary, you can also purchase canned or dry prescription diets from veterinarians to feed dogs with kidney disease, heart and other conditions.

As for bones, our best advice is caution. Some bones (such as poultry or pork bones) are absolutely discouraged, because they tend to splinter into needlelike fragments that can cause serious damage to the dog's mouth, throat or intestinal tract. Any bone, in fact, once chewed into small pieces, can potentially obstruct the intestines. Ingested bone fragments can also produce a bout of uncomfortable constipation. You're better off leaving them out of your dog's diet altogether.

There are other ways to satisfy a dog's craving to chew. We recommend trying a dense rubber toy specifically designed for this purpose. But if you feel you must give bones to your dog, choose large, hard ones like knuckle or marrow bones. Cook the bone first to destroy harmful organisms, and then carefully monitor its fate so you can remove the bone as soon as it begins to splinter or disintegrate.

Bathing and Grooming

Young puppies are intrigued by life itself. From the moment their eyes open, they develop into world class explorers. Puppies abandon themselves so joyously in their travels that cleanliness becomes difficult to enforce.

Don't get frustrated. Use this opportunity to get the puppy accustomed to being handled for bathing and grooming. In fact, start the day you get it home. Purchase the appropriate comb or brush for your breed's coat and practice its use early and often. Make a habit of touching the puppy's feet and nails several times each day. This will help reduce the dog's anxiety at nail-trimming time. Also, run your hands over the coat and gently fuss with the hair around the eyes and ears. These may need frequent cleaning or plucking in the future.

Many people wonder how often a dog needs to be bathed. The answer depends on the breed, the kind of life the dog leads and whether it has a skin disorder. In general, dogs need only be bathed when dirty (or when a medicated shampoo is prescribed). More frequent shampooing may dry out the coat. When the proper shampoo and grooming techniques are employed, as they are in the case of show dogs (who are bathed very often), the results can be quite spectacular.

Let's begin with basic grooming tools. Used correctly, these

Canine children are like human children when it comes to staying clean. Just ask any breeder about weaning a litter. And while young puppies are admittedly messy, they're also wonderfully funny about it. Take advantage of that untidy tyke and get it accustomed to grooming and bathing early on. *Diane Keeler*

tools contribute significantly to the health of the skin and hair and enhance a dog's general appearance.

1. *Brushes* come in a wide variety of sizes and styles. The bristle brush is an all-purpose brush that may be used on short-, medium-, double-coated and long-coated breeds. The bristles can be made of nylon, natural material or a combination of the two. The last is the most popular variety. It combines reasonable price with flexibility, as it can be used on many different coat types. All-nylon bristles are quite hard. They may break fragile hair or cause static electricity, so they are inappropriate for some types of coats. The softest type of brush is a natural bristle brush. It is also the most expensive.

The younger a puppy is when its grooming routine is established, the better it will accept grooming as an adult. This becomes even more important for dogs of deep-coated or heavily groomed breeds, such as this Old English Sheepdog puppy.

F. Earl Rich

As with other features of grooming, regular nail trimming is essential and must be started very early. Indeed, most breeders start trimming nails soon after birth. Accepting attention to nails and feet is important for all puppies to learn, especially to breeds who, like this Labrador Retriever, grow large enough to make an effective resistance.

Judith McClung

Pin brushes are usually used to groom long-haired breeds such as Afghans, Lhasa Apsos, Shih Tzu and Yorkshire Terriers. They are also good for double-coated breeds like the Old English Sheepdog. A variety of sizes are available for easy brushing of small, medium and large breeds. The pin palm brush, an oval rubber pad with pins that have rounded tips to prevent coat damage, is a special brush used to groom the face and legs of hard-coated terriers.

A common type of brush is the slicker brush. The bent-wire teeth of the slicker brush are set close together to help remove mats and dead hair. Most come in three sizes: small, for Toy breeds; medium, for average-sized breeds; and large, for heavy-coated or large breeds. Slicker brushes will take out large amounts of coat, which is good if you want to reduce the around-the-house accumulation from shedding. A slicker may not be the correct choice if you're trying to keep the maximum amount of coat on your dog for the show ring.

All-rubber brushes have flexible, short, soft bristles with rounded ends. They are fine for polishing the coat of smooth-coated breeds or for removing dead hair without scratching the skin.

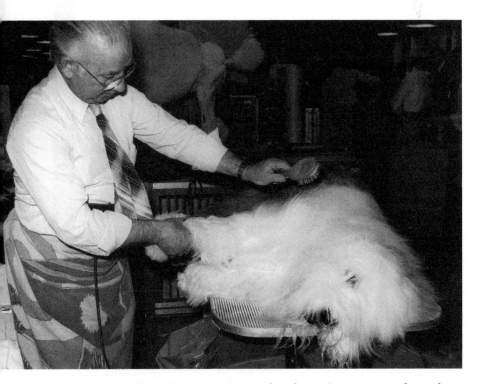

Heavy-coated dogs that compete in the show ring must undergo long grooming sessions. These dogs are often trained to lie on their sides during the process. This makes the whole procedure easier for dog and groomer and is a simple control exercise to teach any dog. *Hamilton Rowan*

Helping you find the right grooming tools and supplies for your dog and showing you how to use them is the business of your puppy's breeder. Add another reason to the growing list of why it's smart to buy from a breeder.

2. *Combs* come in a wide variety of sizes and styles, with different tooth lengths and spacing. In general, fine-tooth combs are best used on soft, silky or sparse hair. Medium-tooth combs are used for average coat textures and coarse-tooth combs are good for dense or heavy coats. Some combs have close-set teeth on one end and wide-spaced teeth on the other end. The length of the teeth should depend on how far the comb needs to penetrate to reach the skin. Some combs have handles; others do not. The best combs are made of stainless steel or chrome-plated solid brass and have spring-tempered teeth with rounded tips to prevent skin irritation.

3. *Stripping implements* are used to groom show terriers and other harsh-coated breeds. In the broadest sense, stripping involves the removal of dead hair using a specialized grooming technique. Many purists insist on plucking with finger and thumb and use stripping tools only to fine tune their work. Clipping these breeds, which cuts off the ends of the hair without removing the dead undercoat, is undesirable because it tends to soften the texture of the coat and sometimes leads to faded coat color.

There are also stripping combs, knives, dressers and undercoat knives. Proper coat stripping is done over a period of weeks, depending on the coat texture, growth pattern, climate and humidity, among other things. For a better explanation on using stripping tools, consult your breed experts.

4. *Hair dryers* speed up the drying process and add a more finished look to the final grooming of long-haired dogs. Many types of hair dryers are on the market, priced from under a hundred dollars to over a thousand. A few examples include portable or hand-held dryers, floor dryers (these are mounted on a stand) and cage dryers, which may be mounted with brackets on a cage door.

Different coats require different drying techniques for the best results. Some breeds are fluff dried with the proper brush.

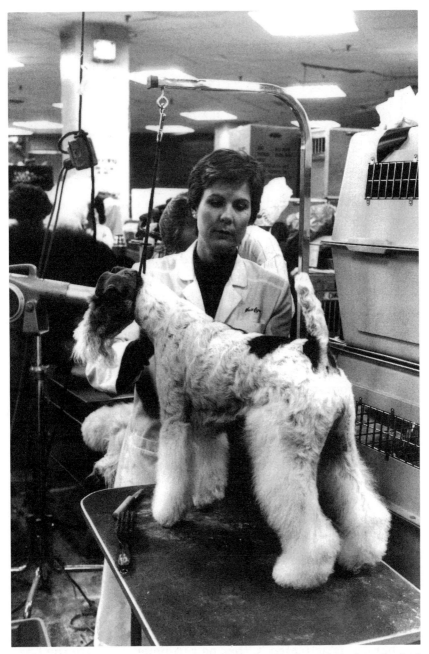

Most terriers and a number of other breeds need to be stripped or plucked to maintain the texture and color of their coats. This is less important if the dog is to be a pet. Special tools and techniques come into play, making hand-stripping a very artful, demanding practice.   *Jennifer Goerk*

Others are massaged with the fingertips to maintain the correct texture. A little research into your breed's coat characteristics should help you decide which process is best for your dog.

Dryers designed for animal use are generally safe and sturdy; most have variable settings for air temperature and are equipped with thermostats to prevent overheating. It is always wise, however, to oversee their use. Be especially careful if you use a small hand-held dryer, which can emit very forceful, very hot air.

5. *Grooming tables,* for the person seriously interested in doing a proper grooming job, come in several sizes and shapes. The table should be sturdy and have a nonskid rubber top. Some are portable and can be folded up for storage. Others have hydraulic mechanisms to let you raise and lower the table. Most professional groomers attach a grooming post and loop to the table. The loop is placed around the dog's neck to keep it from moving around or jumping off the table, although the dog is never left unattended. Whatever type of table is used, grooming should be a comfortable experience for the dog. This shouldn't be too difficult if it is allowed time to adjust to the procedure.

6. *Nail trimmers* come in a variety of types. The most common nail trimmer is the guillotine trimmer. The tip of the dog's nail is inserted into the opening of this metal tool above the cutting blade. When the handles are squeezed together, the cutting mechanism is activated. Other nail trimmer types are the scissors type and the safety nail trimmer, which is equipped with a safety stop near the cutting blade to limit the amount of nail trimmed. Then there are nail files and electric nail trimmers.

Used properly, a small, hand-held hair dryer can give a dog a nice finished look and shorten the after-bath grooming session. It is also helpful to do as the pros do and conduct all your grooming on a table of some kind. A proper grooming table is a wise investment in the good care of your dog.

Nails seem to grow at different rates in different dogs. In any case, one rule holds true: the nails must be kept short for the feet to remain healthy. Long nails interfere with the dog's gait, making walking awkward or painful. They can also break easily. This usually happens at the base of the nail, where blood vessels and nerves are located, and precipitates a trip to the veterinarian.

Another problem affects dogs whose overgrown nails curl toward the foot, eventually piercing the sensitive pads and causing deep pad infections. Dewclaws most frequently become overgrown, presumably because owners commonly overlook them. Many breeders routinely have dewclaws removed when puppies are a few days old. Check your puppy when you get it. If its dewclaws are intact, you must be sure to keep the nails short at all times. These problems can be easily prevented with regular nail care.

To begin with, regularly stroke the puppy's feet, gently touching each toe in turn. Allow it to become accustomed to having this delicate part of the body handled, so it won't be apt to panic when you get down to business later.

Unfortunately, some dogs never adjust to having their nails trimmed. They need only see the clipper and they're squalling, long before you're anywhere near a nail. In that case, trimming nails becomes a two-person job: one person to hold the dog, the other to do the work. It can still be a test of wills. That's why you should accustom your young puppy to nail care. It increases the likelihood of maintaining peace when the animal is fully grown.

Unpigmented nails are simple to trim. If your dog has at least one unpigmented nail, examine it closely. You should see a small pink triangle extending from the base of the nail narrowing toward the tip. This triangle houses the blood supply and nerves, which you want to avoid when trimming the nail. Position the nail trimmer so that it clearly bypasses the pink area, and proceed to clip. That's all there is to nail trimming.

Of course, trimming nails is infinitely more challenging in dogs with black or pigmented nails. Because you can't see the pink part, you must estimate how much nail to clip. To be on the safe side, trim only the part of each nail which hooks downward. The trimmed nail should just clear the floor.

If you're absolutely unnerved at the thought of nail trimming, find a veterinarian or groomer to do it for you. This service usually costs very little and goes a long way in keeping your dog comfortable.

7. *Electric clippers* are specifically designed for home grooming or heavy-duty professional use. They come with a set of blades for different degrees of trimming. The blades are either snapped or screwed into place.

Most dogs trimmed at home with electric clippers don't emerge with a salon-perfect coat. However, these practical tools make it relatively simple to keep many long-haired breeds comfortable, especially in summer.

8. *Scissors* and *shears* are used primarily for trimming and sculpting the coat. Many types are available; the type you need depends on the coat and the desired look. Check your breed literature for more specific instructions. *Warning*: you must be extremely careful, especially with puppies, if you decide to use these grooming tools. The dividing line between hair and skin is often difficult to see, particularly behind the ears and on the underside. A costly mistake can happen in the blink of an eye. If the subject resists your efforts, don't take a chance. Leave this job to a professional groomer.

How to Bathe a Dog

The average dog should be bathed as seldom as possible, only when clearly dirty or smelly. Frequent washing tends to remove natural oils and may cause the coat to become dry and harsh. There are exceptions, however. Dogs who suffer from skin conditions sometimes respond to frequent treatments with a prescription shampoo. And regular bathing or dipping may be necessary during certain times of the year to combat fleas. In any case, here's a primer on dog bathing.

Before shampooing, thoroughly brush the dog to remove dirt, dandruff and dead hair. Brushing also helps to distribute natural oils through the coat. Short- or smooth-coated dogs need only a light stroking with a bristle brush. Take a moment to massage the skin and coat with your fingertips; this helps loosen dead hair and debris (it probably helps relax the dog as well).

Preparing a long-haired dog for bathing is slightly more complicated, since this type of coat is often matted. You must remove mats *before shampooing* or else they trap soap residue. Mats are also harder to remove after a bath.

If there are just a few mats, gently tease them apart with your fingers, the teeth of a comb or a dematting tool. Keep a firm grasp on the hair nearest to the dog's body to prevent pulling on the skin as you work. Soaking the mat in a detangling lotion may also help.

In the case of numerous mats, however, the kindest thing to do is to clip the hair short—and then closely monitor the coat in the future. Mats can form surprisingly fast in places where there is natural body friction, such as at the base of the ears and around the joints. Also, long-haired breeds shedding out the soft puppy coat may be especially prone to matting. Whether you like it or not, if your dog's coat gets matted, it's because you neglected it.

Before you take scissors to your dog's mats, be warned. Many people inadvertently cut their dog's skin while trying to cut out mats. If you must snip, try teasing a comb under the mat so that the teeth rest safely between the skin and the tangle. Then cut the mat off outside the comb. This will create an unsightly gouge in the coat, but at least the mat problem will be solved.

Once all mats are removed and the hair is well brushed, you're ready to place the dog in a tub or sink, depending on size, and start scrubbing.

First, select a shampoo designed *for dogs*, not people. Such products are formulated to clean and condition the dog's more alkaline skin and hair. Baby shampoo or a coconut-oil shampoo will do in a pinch. Gently insert a cotton ball in your dog's ears, and place a dab of mild ophthalmic ointment (like boric acid) or mineral oil in its eyes. You'd best don a plastic apron to protect your clothes or put on your bathing suit, if your dog is large enough for the tub. Now adjust the water temperature, put the dog in the tub, and you're ready to go.

Bathing a dog is much easier if the faucet is equipped with a hose, especially one with a spray nozzle. Wet the hair thoroughly. You can start at either the head or the tail, unless you're using a flea shampoo, in which case you'll want to begin at the head and leave a ring of shampoo on the neck to prevent fleas from fleeing to the head for refuge.

Rinse the hair first to remove as much dirt as possible. Then apply a small amount of shampoo to the back and work up a lather. Don't use too much shampoo, or rinsing will be difficult. Massage the shampoo well all over the body, unless the dog has long hair, in which case you will want to squeeze the shampoo gently through the strands to avoid tangling up the hairs. Don't forget to shampoo the areas under the legs and tail, as well as the head.

Getting water all the way down to skin level requires considerable effort in breeds with heavy coats. In many cases, this is a direct consequence of selective breeding to create an animal with a coat capable of protection against the elements. Unfortu-

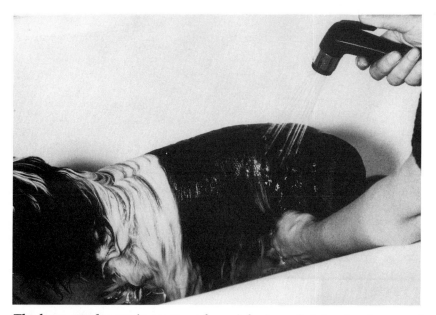

The hose attachment in most modern sinks is perfect for dousing a coat or rinsing out shampoo. In this way a dog is not forced to stand in dirty water. *Shirlee Kalstone*

Take care to prevent the dog from shaking itself during the bath. This Cairn Terrier can get almost as much water on the bather as the bather can put on it. *William C. Freeman*

nately, this means more work at bath time. Be certain to thoroughly douse the dog and work shampoo all the way through to the skin.

Rinsing, too, is more of a chore with a heavily coated breed. Rinsing shampoo from the coat is simpler if your hose attachment releases a fine spray. Check the water temperature again and begin to rinse, starting at the head and finishing at the tail. Make sure all of the soap, especially on the underside of the dog, is gone. You may need to repeat the bathing process two or even three times, depending on the coat length, type and degree of soiling before cleanliness is achieved. For best results, do not fill the tub or sink.

And bather, beware: as soon as a dog gets wet, it has an insidious, devil-may-care urge to shake itself dry. Even a small terrier can spray enough water far enough away to necessitate having a mop handy. If the weather permits, outdoor bathing will greatly minimize the mess of dog washing. Dogs are also less apt to shake if you maintain physical contact with them until you're ready to either grab a towel or take a quick step back.

When you're convinced that the dog is completely rinsed, squeeze excess water from the coat and wrap your dog in an absorbent towel. Take it out of the washtub and blot as dry as possible. Try not to rub the coat dry, since this may only produce tangles. Then let the dog dry in the sun or turn to an electric hair dryer for a quick finish.

Dealing with Skunk Odor

It's true that tomato juice, applied full strength to the coat, deadens the obnoxious odor of skunk. Nothing works 100 percent, however. Repeated baths (outdoors, if at all possible) may be necessary. If you share your habitat with many skunks, ask your breeder or local dog club for suggestions about coping with this problem.

Special bathing products sold by veterinarians and pet stores can also help eliminate skunk odor. Eventually, the lingering aroma dissipates on its own. Forget about saving the dog's collar, leash or other accoutrements worn at the time of the assault, though. Skunk odor will waft from these articles far longer than you can stand it, so just consider them casualties of war and retire them to the trash.

In any altercation with a skunk, the dog is never the odds-on favorite. If skunks are prevalent in your location, be sure you know how to get rid of the odor if your dog should get sprayed. *Judy Sullivan*

Brushing Your Dog's Teeth

Dental hygiene is often ignored in the dog. The outcome? Consider what your teeth might look and feel like after months, years or even a lifetime of neglect. They'd be a wreck, and you'd be miserable. Yes, canine teeth also need frequent brushing to prevent gum disease and early tooth loss, as well as just plain foul breath.

Despite the popular conception, dog biscuits and bones do not keep the teeth clean and healthy. Although some veterinarians feel that gnawing on these hard substances has benefit, it does not prevent the buildup of plaque and tartar which, unless removed, can lead to gum inflammation, tooth root abscesses and other oral problems. That's the simple truth.

The teeth should be brushed at least once or twice a week, more often if possible. As with grooming, acclimation is best started early in the puppy's life.

To make a toothbrush, fold a square gauze pad loosely around the tip of your index finger. Or you can use a small, soft child's toothbrush or buy a special toothbrush from a veterinarian. Dip the toothbrush or gauze pad in a toothpaste designed for dogs (not for humans, since human formulations can upset the dog's stomach) or into a paste made of baking soda and water. Next, vigorously scrub the outside surfaces of the teeth, especially the rear teeth. With the gauze pad, you may also try to gently massage the gums. It is not necessary to brush the interior surfaces of the teeth.

Your veterinarian should check your dog's mouth for tooth or gum disease during annual checkups. The most common

Just as with people, a dog's teeth are meant to last a lifetime. A regular routine of dental hygiene will keep your dog's mouth clean, healthy and trouble-free, and most of the work can be done at home by the owner.

problem, tartar accumulation, resembles yellow or brown cement deposits along the gumline or in the crevices of the teeth. Despite your best efforts, a proper dental cleaning under general anesthesia may need to be performed periodically in a veterinarian's office.

Certain breeds commonly retain their baby teeth, especially the canines. In that case, duplicate sets of teeth are seen in the dog's mouth after approximately six months of age. Retained baby teeth can cause malocclusion, since they prevent adult teeth from growing into their correct positions. Retained baby teeth are often extracted by a veterinarian.

Anal Sacs

Finally, a word about anal sacs. These two sacs are located in the muscle tissue on either side of the anus at the five and seven o'clock positions. An intensely malodorous secretion, usually brownish and watery in appearance, resides within the sacs.

The anal sac fluid, which emerges through two tiny ducts, serves an unknown purpose in the dog. It may help dogs mark territory or enable them to distinguish one another's sexual identity, according to different theories. Whatever their raison d'être, the anal sacs of most dogs can be ignored throughout life. Other dogs, however, are bothered by periodic anal sac problems. They show it by madly dragging their hindquarters across the floor or biting and licking at the tail area. These dogs need to have their anal sacs manually emptied (expressed). A few need to have the sacs surgically removed.

How often may your dog's anal sacs need to be expressed? This depends on whether your dog is one who suffers from bouts of impaction or from actual anal sac infections. Some dogs need monthly attention, while others can go several months without a problem. This is best discussed with your veterinarian, especially if anal sac impaction affects your dog. Should you feel you want to empty the anal sacs at home, here are some guidelines.

Begin by standing the dog on a firm surface. The floor will do fine with a large dog, while a table (with surface protected) may be necessary to express the sacs of a small dog. Hold a piece of cotton or paper towel in one hand to cover the anal area. This is useful because the secretion usually squirts out from the ducts once pressure is applied over the sacs.

With the absorbent material in place, put your thumb on one side of the anus and your index finger on the other. Gently squeeze your fingers together until the contents of the sacs begin to emerge from the ducts. Usually, the secretion is quite watery, but if it's been retained for a while, it may resemble toothpaste. Don't use excessive force, or you may rupture the delicate sacs.

Another method of expressing the anal sacs involves inserting your gloved and lubricated forefinger into the anus and feeling for each anal sac individually within the sphincter muscle. Then, grasping it between your thumb and finger, gently press on the sac until the fluid is released. This procedure should not be painful but it may be uncomfortable for the dog, so you'll probably need somebody to hold the animal.

If you find that the secretion won't budge, first try redirecting the pressure. Occasionally, the sacs will be completely impacted and then it's time to see the veterinarian. This also holds true for secretion containing pus or blood, which indicates an infection of the anal sacs. If not treated promptly, they could become abscessed, which is very painful. Anal sac infections are frequently treated with oral and local antibiotics. The latter is inserted through the ducts into the anal sacs themselves.

Anal sac problems are an annoying minor condition that affects some dogs. Fortunately, most dogs are never troubled at all, but for those that are the preceding discussion may be helpful.

Picking a Veterinarian

You and the puppy will make frequent visits to the veterinarian in the first few months, so it's extremely important to find someone you trust. If you're not familiar with the practitioners in your area, word-of-mouth is a good place to start. Listen closely to what people say about their experiences with local veterinarians. What pleases or distresses one person may have the opposite effect on you.

For instance, your neighbor may dislike a large clinic nearby because she never seems to see the same doctor twice. She wants a smaller practice, perhaps one or two doctors, where she and her dog receive personal attention.

You, however, may discover that the clinic has lots of doctors because it is a teaching facility. Its senior veterinarians have advanced training, are highly skilled and know the latest medical information—they must, because they pass the information on to the interns and residents who are part of the examination, diagnostic and treatment processes. This degree of sophistication may be exactly what makes you feel secure. To each his own.

Wherever you go, you must respect and feel comfortable with the veterinarian who cares for your dog's health. Don't forget that the animal, though it broadcasts many clues to the educated eye, can't speak for itself. This makes you a vital part of the examination process. Only you can relate the important details of your pet's health. And when it comes to illness, only you can describe the problem's onset, signs and so on. You must effectively communicate with your dog's veterinarian, not feel intimidated or shy. If an individual's personality puts you off or otherwise hinders your ability to tell the full story, then find another vet.

Useful things you might want to know about local veterinarians include whether emergency service is provided at night and on weekends, or whether an emergency clinic in the vicinity provides emergency coverage. Some veterinarians hold evening or weekend appointments; perhaps this fits in with your lifestyle. Furthermore, if you intend to travel frequently, ask if the animal hospital accepts boarders.

It's important to know if the practice you're considering is "full-service," meaning that the practitioners can handle a broad spectrum of cases. Are specialists available for consultation, or are certain procedures referred to specialists elsewhere? Don't be embarrassed to inquire about the type of equipment on hand. Are X-ray machinery, ultrasound and dental equipment, for example, available? Many up-to-date practices now employ a computer system for organized record keeping and also for sending you timely reminders for vaccinations or other important procedures. This may represent a major convenience to you.

Although you may not have the opportunity to meet the doctors, try to visit a clinic in which you're interested. At least, you can form a general impression of the facility and its staff.

Beginning a Program of Good Health

Vaccinations

Most puppies receive their first vaccination at eight weeks of age, although some breeders or pet stores vaccinate their puppies a few weeks earlier. The first vaccination is usually a "combination" shot, intended to produce immunity against five serious canine diseases: distemper, hepatitis, leptospirosis, parvovirus and parainfluenza. Different veterinarians use different vaccination schedules, but in general, this DHLPP shot is repeated twice more, at two- to four-week intervals. Until the three-shot series is completed, it's best to isolate your puppy from unfamiliar dogs, since the proper degree of immunity is not yet established. Once the puppy has received the last of the three shots, usually by twelve to sixteen weeks of age, it's safe for it to come in contact with strange dogs. The vaccination is updated with an annual booster.

Most veterinarians administer the first rabies vaccination when a dog is six months old. The next rabies shot is given in a year. Ask your veterinarian if the vaccination needs to be boosted each year or once every three years throughout the dog's adult life. The rabies vaccine is an absolute requirement for licensing your dog. Many towns offer a free rabies clinic yearly. Check with your town officials.

Two other vaccinations are available for dogs at the present time for the prevention of tracheobronchitis (kennel cough) and coronavirus infection, which can cause a hemorrhagic gastroenteritis. These vaccinations are usually administered twice, spaced a few weeks apart. Ask your veterinarian whether these

Smooth Fox Terrier. *Lisa Sachs*

Veterinary science makes constant strides forward in the knowledge of animal health. Today, your puppy can be protected by sophisticated vaccinations that provide potent protection against diseases that, earlier in the century, wiped out whole populations of dogs. With good management and a sensible program of boosters, most dogs can be expected to live long, happy, healthful lives.

Golden Retrievers (right). *Joanne Bartley*

vaccinations are considered an important part of your dog's disease protection.

At the time of this writing, a vaccination for Lyme disease is under intense investigation and has been approved for use in some states. Again, refer to your veterinarian for updated information about this important vaccine.

Gastrointestinal Parasites

The majority of puppies contract some form of internal parasite either before or shortly after birth. Although this may sound repulsive to you, it's a normal part of being a dog. There is no need to be excessively concerned, provided you have your puppy checked and treated promptly. Left untreated, intestinal parasites can cause serious harm.

Therefore, it's essential to bring along a small, fresh sample of your puppy's stool when you make your first veterinary visit. When the stool is dissolved, eggs or parasites from this sample will be clearly visible under a microscope. Do not assume your puppy has no intestinal parasites simply because no worms have shown up in the stool. Adult worms often live exclusively within the intestinal tract; the tiny eggs they release serve as the only clue to their existence. Furthermore, other internal parasites, even as mature organisms, never reach a size visible to the naked eye. Let your veterinarian discover which type, if any, of these parasites inhabits your puppy's system and treat it accordingly.

Deworming is often as simple as administering small amounts of palatable oral medication. In some cases, however, injections are necessary. You'll be asked to submit samples of your dog's stool throughout its life to ensure that it has not been exposed to any new or recurring parasites.

Heartworms

Another parasite you'll learn about during your puppy's first visit to the veterinarian is heartworm.

The microscopic heartworm initially gains entry to the dog's body through the bite of an infected mosquito. Later, adult worms inhabit the heart's chambers where, now several inches long, they present a life-threatening problem. We'll go over heartworms in more detail in chapter VIII. Suffice it to say for now that veterinarians dispense preventative drugs to protect dogs whenever mosquitoes are active in the local environment. In some parts of the country, this is virtually year-round. Elsewhere, it is a seasonal problem. In all cases, however, owners should have their dogs' blood tested yearly to confirm that heartworm infection has not occurred. If a dog tests positive, it can be treated, but the treatment and its aftermath are extremely stressful.

Spaying or Neutering

Your veterinarian should initiate a discussion about spaying or neutering at the time of your first appointment, months in advance of the actual surgery. If he or she doesn't, then inquire. It's a good time to start thinking about whether you want to spay or neuter your pet for preventative health care, birth control and to avoid some potentially undesirable behavior. Remember, however, that these surgical procedures render a dog ineligible to compete in the show ring.

Many breeders offer pet quality puppies for sale with the stipulation that the dogs be neutered or spayed when they reach the appropriate age. This is the breeder's way of insuring breed improvement, by only allowing high-quality dogs to reproduce.

For your dog's sake, for all dogs' sake and for your sake, arrange to have your pet spayed or neutered. Ask your veterinarian when it will be appropriate and act accordingly. Your dog will be just as lovely a companion, maybe better, and you will know that your dog will never be a factor in today's tragic population explosion among companion animals.

Sigrid C. Reisiger

You, of course, think your puppy is absolutely perfect. And it is—for you, and as a pet, but perhaps not as a model for future members of its breed.

Possibly the best reason to have your female spayed while she is young (most veterinarians recommend six months of age) is for its health benefit. Mammary gland cancer is much more common in an unspayed (intact) female. If your puppy is spayed before her first heat (at six months, for example), her risk of developing breast tumors is substantially reduced. The odds are still in her favor, though diminished, if she is spayed after her first heat. But if you wait until she reaches maturity, say after her second or third heat, the operation will not reduce her risk of breast cancer. This is why it is important to have her spayed early in life.

Other reasons? The surgery itself, complete removal of the

uterus and both ovaries, is ordinarily quicker and less hemorrhagic in immature females, so the risk of complications is reduced. Owners are spared the stress of having to confine the
female who, when she comes into season, sends out enticing
messages to male dogs in the vicinity. Furthermore, because the
reproductive organs are gone, spaying eliminates the possibility
of unwanted pregnancy as well as the regular heat period when
dogs leave blood-tinged stains on carpets and furniture. Lastly,
the potential infections, cancers and other problems involving
the uterus and/or ovaries are eliminated along with these organs.

Diseases of the male reproductive organs related to the presence of male hormones are not unknown, either. Although neutering represents an advantage as far as prevention is concerned,
this is not usually the primary reason owners have their dogs
castrated.

Most people want their dog to be neutered because they
think it helps make him a better pet. This may be true, for the
following reasons: Intact male dogs can act aggressively toward
other dogs and people because they are trying to protect and
control their territory. In the male mind, "territory" may be
your property, its toys, females in heat, a bowl of food and so
on. This type of behavior is unacceptable to most people and
may be strongly influenced by the dog's male hormones. Neutering a dog with aggressive tendencies at an early age may
reduce these problems. Castration is also recommended for aggressive older dogs, although its chance for success is less certain.

A neutered dog has less temptation to roam, too, as well as
fight. He probably won't embarrass you at important dinner
parties by seeking romance with your company's legs. And just
as important, he won't contribute to the already burgeoning
population of homeless puppies, something we should all be
ashamed of.

Let's face it. Spaying and neutering dogs who are not intended for breeding or for the show ring is simply the all-round
right thing to do. We hope you will choose to have it performed
for a happier, healthier pet.

Owning a dog is a privilege as well as a pleasure. The conscientious owner knows that with the privilege comes the responsibility of keeping the dog under control. *Barbara Turner*

▪4▪

LIVING WITH YOUR DOG

Being a Good Neighbor

Their world may not extend beyond a couple of blocks. Nevertheless, dogs are an integral part of society. As a dog owner, you have a serious responsibility. You must mold your dog into a good neighbor—not a nuisance or a menace. Left to its own devices, a dog naturally might enjoy destroying someone's precious lawn, chasing other animals or having a loud dialogue with the midnight moon. These and lots of other behaviors your neighbors will hate, of course, never strike your dog as anything but fun, unless it is properly trained and supervised. This is your responsibility. Certainly you don't want your dog's behavior to become a point of contention between otherwise compatible neighbors.

To begin with, no dog should be allowed to roam indiscriminately. Most people are reluctant to confront the owner of an offending dog, but no one appreciates canine trespassing. Dogs lacking human supervision will often leave destruction in their path, and you are liable for your pet's activities. Don't let bad feelings start because you have given your dog a free rein.

Furthermore, you put your dog's life at risk every time you allow it such freedom. Your pet may attack or be attacked by other animals—wild (think about rabies) or domesticated. Chances are, at some point, the dog will be hit and perhaps killed by a car. A free-roaming dog is more susceptible to picking up parasites and disease. And it may simply disappear one day, leaving you to wonder whether it has been abducted or killed. Sadly, these are common occurrences.

If you want to keep your dog outdoors, an exercise run or a sturdy fence around your yard is mandatory. Hopefully, if your dog is a barker, your neighbors live a good distance away. However, in the densely populated urban and suburban areas in which most of us live, it is simply unacceptable to permit a dog to bark endlessly. You are going to have extremely unhappy neighbors. Breaking the barking habit can be a real problem; you can try working with a trainer to come up with a solution, or you may simply have to keep the dog indoors. Certainly, it is unfair to make other people suffer while you're away.

In today's lifestyle, part of being a thoughtful dog owner is keeping your dog on its own property. A fenced yard or exercise area and on-leash walks are better for people and dogs than allowing animals to roam at large. Dogs should always be a substantial pleasure, never a potential menace. *Terry Smith*

Every well-cared-for dog has the potential to be a canine goodwill ambassador. From puppyhood on, all dogs should be raised and trained to promote the real and important image of the dog as the friend of man.

Remember, barking is both natural for dogs and a learned behavior in certain situations. To correct unwanted barking, you must catch the dog in the act and administer a stern, forceful correction. You cannot correct undesirable behavior unless the dog is actually caught in the act of performing it.

Many dogs dig under or leap over fences, so you will have to discover your dog's style of escape artistry and foil it. If expense is not a problem, you may want to think about an "invisible fence," where an underground electric wire is placed around the perimeter of your property. When the current is turned on, a signal is emitted from a small box worn on your dog's collar. The dog learns, after a short training period, to interpret the signal as a warning not to cross the property line. If the animal ignores the signal, a small shock is delivered through little prongs on the inside of the collar box. Though not nearly enough to injure, this acts as a strong deterrent. Most dogs learn so quickly what the signal means after a short training period that they never reach the shock phase.

Many dogs respond well to the invisible fence. Of course, it works strictly one-way: it does not prevent other dogs or animals from entering your property. Installation is not cheap (and

may be unavailable in some parts of the country), but invisible fencing provides an option for people who abhor an obstructed view of the world yet want to prevent their own dog from encountering dangers beyond the property line.

Water and shelter must be made available for dogs kept outdoors, especially in very hot or cold weather. Be sure that the water supply has not evaporated or frozen. No matter what kind of coat your dog has, shade must be provided from the sun during summer months. And obviously, some dogs with thin or short coats were not designed for living outdoors in areas where winter weather can be harsh. If your dog is sufficiently coated and you want it to spend time outdoors in winter, it still needs adequate shelter from moisture, cold and wind.

In fact, the vast majority of companion dogs live almost exclusively indoors. The chances are good your dog will, too. Therefore, most contact with neighbors occurs from the end of a leash. This is when you can best show off your dog's ability to be a good neighbor. The clearest way to demonstrate that your dog has manners is to make sure it knows the basic commands (sit, stay, down, come; see chapter V). Also, exercise *your* command of good manners by removing and disposing properly of your dog's feces. Whether or not this practice is required by law in your area, it makes for a cleaner neighborhood as well as appreciative neighbors.

Exercising Your Dog

The amount of exercise your dog needs depends on age, health, breed and temperament. In general, Sporting, Hound, Working and Herding breeds appreciate and require more exercise than

other breeds, especially the larger dogs. In fact, if denied sufficient exercise, they may become frustrated and turn to destruc-
tiveness as a way of venting energy. How much time you have
for dog-related activities is obviously something to be considered before you decide on a breed.

Young animals always seem more keen on vigorous exercise
than older animals. In the first few months of life, don't be
surprised if your puppy has tremendous spurts of energy, followed by extensive rest periods. This is natural for this stage of
life.

Maintaining a regular exercise schedule for your dog as it
grows will help it stay fit and healthy. Compared to their ancestors, today's dogs are out of condition; many are considerably
overweight by the time they reach early adulthood because of
too much rich food and too little exercise. Obesity, in turn, leads
to all sorts of problems. Keep tabs on your dog's weight and
muscle tone. You should be able to just feel the dog's ribs as you
stand over it and pass your hands down the rib cage.

What kinds of exercises can you do with your dog? Walking
is only the start. If your dog is well trained, it can be taken off
lead in public areas like parks and fields, and work off as much
steam as it likes. Always check first with public authorities to
see what the local laws allow. Perhaps you have friends, rela-
tives or acquaintances whose property you can use for the same
purpose.

You can also take your dog hiking, jogging or swimming.
Dogs enjoy chasing balls and retrieving sticks or Frisbees. For
more structured activity, maybe you'd like to get involved with
field trial, obedience or tracking work, or hunt with your dog.

German Shepherd Dog. *Tom Morrissette*

The essential matter of exercise: Dogs are usually active individuals and, given the opportunity, will exercise themselves or join you in physical pursuits in a number of ways. Regular, on-lead road work has enhanced the fluid movement of this German Shepherd. The Cairn Terriers in hot pursuit of the same ball give off an unmistakable aura of energy, and the Golden is fulfilling part of its heritage, getting wonderful physical conditioning and enjoying quality time with its young owner all at once.

Cairn Terriers. *Wanda Clark*

Golden Retriever. *Lane Peacock*

The AKC can help put you in touch with representatives of local clubs devoted to these activities.

Above all, dogs just want to spend time with the people they love. It's up to you to make that time count.

Some animals can't tolerate a lot of exercise because of hip dysplasia, arthritis or other medical conditions. These problems may occur even in young dogs. If exercise makes your dog sore and lame, or if it collapses or fatigues easily, have your vet examine the animal.

Traveling with Your Dog

If you and your family are looking forward to taking trips with your new puppy, it's best to prepare for the event right from the start.

Car sickness is fairly common in dogs. You can help your puppy overcome this by letting it adjust to car rides early in life. While it's still a few months old, take the puppy out and sit with it in the car. There's no need to start the engine yet. Just let the animal get used to the sights and smells of the automobile. Later there will be less cause for alarm. Many dogs see the inside of a car only on those rare occasions they are driven to the veterinarian. Few dogs enjoy that particular experience. Of course, they're going to panic when the car door closes behind them!

After a few sessions of sitting in the car, the puppy is ready for short trips. Plan to take your puppy out before eating, so it has an empty stomach. You may want to begin by circling the block a few times. Soothe the puppy's excitement or anxiety during these rides, and reward afterwards with praise and treats. Before long, the puppy should think car rides are another part of normal life, and it will be ready for extended trips without incident.

We recommend using the crate when you travel with a dog. Crates can provide protection from serious injury or prevent escape in the event you are involved in an accident. Furthermore, they can prevent trouble by keeping the dog away from the driver's lap and feet.

No matter how much it seems to enjoy it, never allow a dog to ride with its head sticking out the car window. For one thing, eye injuries are likely. Furthermore, you risk losing your dog this way—to escape (even the smallest dog can leap out the window in a flash) or death from trauma once they hit the road. Better safe than sorry; keep your dog away from open windows while you're driving.

Traveling with a dog by air is another consideration. Unless it's a seasoned traveler, your dog will probably find flying stressful, so you may want to think twice before subjecting it to the friendly skies. Each airline seems to have its own rules and regulations for canine passengers. You must check with the airline well in advance of your trip. All will require a regulation crate, however, and some sort of documentation from a veterinarian certifying the dog is in good health.

Many people prefer to tranquilize their dogs prior to travel. Bear in mind, however, that tranquilization may not be absolutely necessary. In fact, because of certain medical considerations, tranquilization may be contraindicated for your dog. Ask your veterinarian for his or her advice in seeing your dog safely to the destination.

Finding a Place to Stay

It can be challenging to find motels, hotels or campgrounds that don't automatically say no to dogs. Always find out in advance whether pets are welcome at your expected destination. The AAA tourbooks list this information, as does the *Touring with*

Towser booklet published by Quaker Professional Services. Occasionally, an establishment makes the decision based on the dog's size or whether you will keep it crated. Again, you can avoid disappointment by checking first.

But if your pet *is* given the green light, respect the privacy of other guests by keeping your dog as quiet as possible. Never leave the dog unattended, since many dogs lose their cool when left alone in a strange place and bark or destroy property. When you're in for the night, confine the dog to the crate. Try to prevent any possibility of "accidents." Remember, the fate of future travelers with their dogs rests on how well you and yours respect the rights of the establishment.

Finally, if the hotel or motel keeper hasn't already told you, ask where you may walk your dog. The management may not appreciate its well-kept grounds used for this purpose. In any case, be sure to scoop up after your dog.

Boarding

Sometimes it's not possible to travel with a dog. Also, bringing the dog on vacation can hamper the activity of the rest of the family. Incidentally, it might be much smarter on your part to board your beloved pet at a reliable kennel than to leave him with a friend or relative or with some sitter. If you decide to leave your dog in a kennel, here are some points to consider.

First of all, check around the neighborhood to see if other dog owners can recommend a particular boarding kennel. Ask if they thought the kennel was clean, well organized and respected any special requests made regarding their dog's food or housing. Or if they didn't like a kennel, find out why. Did the dog contract an illness at the kennel, did it come home filthy or did it suddenly support a small nation of fleas? When it comes to choosing a kennel for your dog, our best advice is to take the recommendation of someone you know who has had a satisfactory experience.

Then make an unannounced stop at the boarding kennel and ask to see the facility. The staff should not find your arrival disturbing and should honor, within reason, your request to view the premises. Expecting total spotlessness is unrealistic, but personnel should be actively cleaning runs, and every dog should have clean water. Foul odors of any kind should not pervade the air. Make a mental note of how the animals, in general, look to you.

Well-run kennels take a minute to check for fleas when dogs arrive and just before they go home; flea problems are immediately treated. They require that all dogs have up-to-date vaccinations, for their own protection and the protection of other dogs. Many kennels require proof of a current kennel cough vaccination before they will admit a dog. The proprietors may insist that you submit a certificate from your veterinarian stating all of these requirements are met, so be prepared well ahead of time. These rules may seem inconvenient to you, but they are in the best interest of your dog.

Kennels should also allow you to bring food or toys from home, and provide canned food instead of dry when asked, for instance. Administering regular medication to dogs may or may not present a problem at a boarding kennel. If it does, it might be better to board your dog at a veterinary hospital, where qualified personnel will see to this job.

It's imperative to leave an emergency number where you can be reached, as well as the name and number of your veterinarian. If telephones and mail service are not part of your vacation plans, provide the name and number of someone whose judgment you trust, and leave written instructions empowering this person to authorize necessary medical treatment. It's also a good idea to compose a brief medical history of your animal and leave it with the kennel staff just in case.

Pomeranian. *Karen A. Nicholson*

Saint Bernard. *Larry Payne*

All dogs require training if they are to live happily with people. Differences in size mean only differences in approach. All dogs should be obedient to basic commands for their safety and comfort, and for the safety and comfort of people around them.

The Gordon Setter was developed in Scotland and is a capable, workmanlike gun dog.

Jeannie Wagner

Perhaps one of the most familiar working roles dogs fill is that of an aide to police work. This group gives every indication that it stands ready to protect its community with great devotion. *Duane Pickel*

In today's world, pointing dogs don't always indicate the location of birds. This alert German Wirehaired Pointer is on the lookout for illegal drugs. *Ivy Ainsworth*

Modern veterinary medicine has made it possible for our dogs to live longer, healthier lives. It is still our responsibility to maintain and safeguard their physical well-being.

David Willman, Tufts University,
School of Veterinary Medicine

The day you bring your new puppy home should be filled with happiness. The breeder wants you to enjoy your new friend for many years and stands ready to help whenever called upon. *Steve Eltinge*

In a well-bred litter, there will be very small differences between show and pet quality puppies. Tell the breeder what kind of dog you want and be guided by his or her knowledge and practical experience. *Elfie Shea*

This Basset Hound and its young friends mirror everything a good dog/human relationship should be. *Sumner W. Fowler*

The Australian Cattle Dog is first and foremost a working dog.

James B. Spencer

The ever-popular Beagle remains the number-one rabbit dog. *Ivy Ainsworth*

The Irish Terrier, mainly a pet and show dog today, has had a variety of functions since he first came into being. *D. Davis*

The Apollo of Dogdom, the Great Dane is a universal favorite and one of the most familiar giant breeds. *J. S. Dorl*

Our dogs often make our good times that much better. This Shih Tzu poses with a girls' band at opening ceremonies of the world dog show in Denmark. *Soren Wesseltoft*

This young bather and his Bearded Collie friend are the picture of happiness. *Shiela Green*

There are special joys that touch the relationship of an old dog and its owner.

A Whippet and a Norwich Terrier in a moment of quiet togetherness.

An English Cocker Spaniel shows just how to handle a water retrieve of a partridge. *D. Davis*

A West Highland White Terrier getting ready for a show ring appearance.
Soren Wesseltoft

A young Whippet enjoying the seashore. *Steve Eltinge*

Dogs often give a special dimension to outdoor activities. Many lovers of the outdoors find their dogs make great backpacking companions.
Kent and Donna Dannen

The sled dog has inspired adventurers and explorers ever since man developed this means of conveyance. The determination on the faces of these Alaskan Malamutes says they mean to get where they are going. *Kent and Donna Dannen*

·5·

TRAINING

You can't live properly with a dog unless it's trained. It's that simple, and it really doesn't matter whether your canine is a four-pound Toy or a 104-pound Working breed. An untrained dog is an invitation to disaster. A dog that won't come when you call is always in danger.

You can't blame the dog either. If you don't train your dog, you are at fault. No one else. In fact, if you're not prepared to properly train your dog, you probably shouldn't get one in the first place.

Now for the good news: dogs are easily trained. That's probably the reason why dogs have long been America's favorite pet. Despite the fact that they train relatively easily, however, you still have to do the job. One way to make training simple is to get a breed that readily adapts to your life-style and that corresponds to what you want in a canine companion. Serious breeders can help you with this. They should tell you about their breed's inherent trainability—advice you should heed before making your final decision.

Rest assured that training does not strip a dog of natural instincts or joie de vivre. After all, these are the things that attract people to dogs in the first place. We want you to *celebrate* the canine spirit, not abuse it.

What training does, however, is structure the dog's responses, giving you a good *companion*. Training gives you an animal you can trust, even flaunt. In fact, it establishes a channel of communication between you and your dog that significantly enhances your mutual respect and friendship.

Every civilized dog should know at least five basic commands: heel, sit, down, stay and come. These commands form the core of the exercises required for a Companion Dog degree in an American Kennel Club Novice Obedience competition. Even if you don't take your dog beyond these beginning lessons, they are absolutely essential in making every dog a true companion.

Incidentally, you train your dog to understand its name in much the same way you train it to do anything—by simple, repetitive action. As far as the name goes make sure everyone in the household is using the same name. And, you *can* teach an older dog a new name, if you must.

Is My Breed Right for Training?

All dogs are suitable for training, although some breeds make naturally superior pupils because generations of ancestors were selected for trainability. (Consult owners, breeders and AKC Standards for information about tractable breeds. Check out an Obedience competition.) If you purchase a breed not known for prowess in the Obedience ring, don't give up. Persevere. If training isn't going so well, maybe it's your problem instead of the dog's. Read through this section; perhaps you'll find that

German Shepherd Dog. *Tracy Simmons*

Golden Retriever. *Carol B. Slider*

A dog can be trained effectively at any age. Often, the best results are achieved by working with young puppies. However, dogs are naturally adaptable and are usually eager to please. Consider the large number of grown dogs that change hands and how these dogs must learn the routines of their new homes. They do adapt, often with great success.

your methods are inconsistent or confusing. If you're at your wit's end, contact a professional trainer for advice or join a local obedience class. Also, you may need to research training and behavior problems more thoroughly. There should be a shelf full of appropriate books at your local library or bookstore. Many fine volumes, written exclusively about dog training, cover subjects beyond the scope of this general discussion.

If you're wondering whether age is an obstacle, rest assured that there is no age limit for effective dog training. You may have to be a little more persistent in training an adult dog, but there is no truth to the adage that "you can't teach an old dog new tricks." However, it is certainly easier if a foundation for learning is initiated right from the start of the relationship.

Working with a Dog's Instincts

One thing that all dogs have in common is a desire to please their owners. Unfortunately, an interspecies language barrier makes it difficult to get the point across. Training lets you overcome this barrier. It establishes a means of communication between you and your dog that's bound to brighten your relationship. After all, training shows your dog how to earn exactly what it craves—your approval.

Before you start actively training your dog, you might want to invest a little time learning a touch of the dog's language. We don't just mean barking. Body language is an extremely important communication tool between dogs and other creatures. If you spend just a few moments watching your dog, you may come away with the ability to understand, even "connect" with your dog, much to its delight.

For instance, dogs often show they want to romp by making a "play bow." You'll recognize a play bow when your dog stretches out his forelegs before him and directs his rear end straight up in the air. Dogs instantly understand what this posture means, whether it is performed by another dog or a human being. Try imitating the play bow in front of your dog when it seems to be in the mood for fun. Chances are, your pet will reward you with an intriguing and exuberant response.

Other forms of canine body language worth understanding are signs of submission and aggression. Dogs who are submissive will often crouch down when you approach them, tuck their tail between their legs or roll over to expose the belly. They may urinate on the floor. This is a dog who doesn't want to assert itself. This dog may need a lot of reassurance. Training may help the submissive dog "find itself."

An aggressive dog, besides showing teeth or letting out a low growl, may indicate aggression by raising the hair on the back, putting the ears forward and holding the tail high. You can usually catch a glimpse of the dog's mood by the ugly look in its eyes.

In fact, reading the expression in a dog's eyes is a powerful way to gauge its feelings, both good and bad. Most dogs do not like to maintain eye contact with a human being or more dominant dog for long; they will shift their gaze sideways before looking back again. In the wild, animals often interpret direct staring as a challenge. Once you build a trusting relationship with a dog, however, you will probably find your dog sending long, loving looks your way without fear of reprisal.

Another thing to remember is that your puppy naturally begins to learn the moment it sets foot in your house, even if you do not know it. Dogs are creatures of habit. They soon establish routines and expectations based on what patterns are set by their owners. Consider the dog who perks up every time it hears a can opener pierce a can lid. Or the one who whines when it sees its owner pick up car keys, because it has learned that soon enough it will be alone for the day. And surely you've seen many a dog surge into action by the sight or sound of a leash being picked up.

All of these are good examples of the power of consistency. Training is really consistently doing the same thing, in the same circumstances, over and over. Expose dogs enough times to predictable signals and they learn to respond accordingly. With obedience training, your goal is to direct this canine ability toward producing desirable behavior. But unlike the examples above, obedience training must be taught in relatively structured, regular sessions.

Eye contact is a potent control factor with any dog. The dominant owner, as "pack leader," has the ability to stare down a dog when circumstances warrant. In a sound happy relationship, human/canine eye contact is most frequently the silent expression of mutual love.

Bearded Collies. *Beth Tilson*

Have confidence in your dog as you set out to train it, and your dog will show confidence in learning. This confidence is established by your consistently responding to a particular action with the same reaction. This means that certain actions are always prohibited, and certain others always encouraged. Vacillation is the deadliest enemy of good training.

Praise and Correction

A well-trained dog knows what it can and cannot do. This is only achieved by consistent reinforcement. A dog that is praised when it does right and corrected when it does wrong will soon learn acceptable behavior.

Praise implies more than obvious approval when your dog has done something right. It also means praising your dog after you have corrected or disciplined it and the dog has responded appropriately, so you can maintain a good relationship. What sort of praise might be considered adequate? Most dogs need no more than a simple "Good dog!" offered in your most supportive, warm voice. Others appreciate a nice pat on the head or neck. Occasionally, a dog will need to be offered some sort of food reward. Start with vocal praise. Your dog will let you know if it gets the message.

Corrections should always be mild and nonviolent. Again, the best tool to use is your own voice. Teach yourself to say "No!" in a loud, firm tone. It needn't be deafening to be effective. Try to leave out panic, anger and just plain annoyance, as these only baffle and disturb the dog.

Many dog owners make a basic, destructive mistake of prolonging their displeasure with a dog who either violates the training or seems slow to learn. You must understand that dogs forget an event after a few minutes; they only know from your reaction that you are unhappy with them. All of which teaches a dog nothing more than you're not so easy to get along with. You've got to catch a dog in the act of doing something wrong, or else *forget about it*. Disciplinary action must be made as fast and be as closely connected with the misdeed as possible for positive results. Holding a grudge is destructive.

Great Dane. *Beth Borgman*

Correct when wrong. Praise when right. It's best to be able to praise your dog immediately after a correction has been made. Just make sure the praise is for correct behavior. Do this no matter how many times you've had to make the identical correction. It takes a few times for any correction to make the right impression. Praise after correction does not lessen the impact of the correction, but it will reassure the dog that you are still friends. You shouldn't have to terrorize a dog in order to produce good results. Remember that the ultimate goal, besides having a well-behaved pet, is to give your dog a chance to please you.

For example, let's look at how you might cope with the common problem of chewing. All puppies have a desire to chew on something, starting from the time they are quite young. It can be a real predicament when the puppy seems to prefer chewing on people or expensive furniture.

The most obvious way to approach this problem is to keep the puppy separated from things it should not chew, whenever you cannot provide supervision. The puppy may need to be crated, for instance, or confined to a "safe" room like the kitchen.

But whenever the puppy is within sight and it takes something unacceptable in its mouth, like your clothing or hand, immediately correct it with a firm "No!" The correction has been adequate if it releases the object from its jaws. As soon as the puppy shows comprehension, turn right around and praise on the spot: "Good dog!" The puppy thus learns that it will be corrected for doing something wrong, but will also receive abundant praise for doing something right.

In most cases, a sufficiently authoritative vocal correction makes the appropriate impression. Just how harsh the correction has to be depends on the reaction of the dog. If the dog is not responding to your correction, chances are you're not being sufficiently commanding. You may need to use a more forceful means of correction (such as a choke or training collar), discussed in more detail below.

There can be a tremendous variation from breed to breed in the degree of firmness necessary to get the proper response from the dog. *Some breeds are far more strong willed and hardheaded than others.* Remember, too, any dog that has been allowed to develop unacceptable habits and is then subjected to correction will always require a stronger hand than one whose owner never allowed it to act that way in the first place.

Never strike your dog, with one possible exception. That exception is when a dog threatens to bite a person. In this case, you'll have to use your own judgment, based on your knowledge of your dog and the circumstances surrounding the incident. If the use of physical force seems warranted, then go with your gut feeling. Afterward, when the situation is under control, it's still advisable to praise the dog—but *only* after the dog is again acting within your orders. Don't take acts of serious aggression anything less than seriously. These dogs absolutely require obedience training if they are going to live to a ripe old age. Consult a veterinarian and trainer for advice in handling the aggressive dog.

Beagle. *Sean Sweeney*

English Springer Spaniel. *Eileen Casper*

A puppy has no concept of what it may or may not chew and, like a human infant, will put anything in its grasp in its mouth. Remember this when you catch your puppy chewing on a forbidden item. Many owners will replace what a dog should not have with something it can have.

And while we're on the subject of praise and correction for aggressive behavior, never try to soothe or comfort a dog who is in the midst of lunging at other animals or people from the end of a leash. It will only reinforce this performance, because you would actually be praising the dog for acting like a monster. A better approach would be to correct the dog, get it under control and *then* offer a few kind words so it will associate praise with civil behavior.

When we say not to hit your dog, we mean using your hand, a newspaper, a stick or anything else. Don't threaten your dog, either. This is almost worse than actually striking it. This is often the cause of "hand-shy" dogs who cringe at the sight of any upraised hand. Some dogs wind up afraid of all human hands, upraised or not. The dog who expects a beating every time it sees an upraised hand has good reason to try to escape to safer ground.

We'll never know why people always seem to associate dog training with rolled-up newspapers. Probably because it's the handiest thing within reach in most households. However, we hope you will resist the temptation to use this "tool." If you think that the sound of the newspaper hitting the dog will frighten the dog into submission, consider this. First of all, training does not occur by scaring a dog into making it do what you want and not do what you find objectionable. Secondly, deliberately teaching a dog to be frightened of loud noises is unwise. What will you do when there's a thunderstorm, for instance, or a display of fireworks? Veterinarians see an awful lot of panic-stricken animals on those occasions, and need to go so far as to tranquilize some of the more extreme cases. If you produce a dog like this, you'll be replacing one problem with another.

A third reason for discouraging you from using a rolled-up newspaper as a training aid is the likelihood of your needing to make a correction someday and finding yourself without one. Remember consistency. The power of correction lies in its immediate administration, not following a lapse of even a few seconds as you traipse around the house looking for ammunition.

You'll notice that we have not used the word "punishment" in our discussion thus far. *A dog is never punished; it is corrected.* This may seem a fine point to you, but in such fine points lie the difference between good and bad dog training.

Take training your dog not to jump on people, for example. The plan: each time the dog leaps up, say "No!" and raise your knee in front of you to disrupt the dog's balance. Next thing the animal knows, it's back on all fours. You say, "Good dog." The lesson is over.

Let's go over what you've done. You've observed the principle of immediate correction, waited for the dog to do what you want and praised it for doing what's right. There's been no unpleasantness from you to the dog: no shouting, no hitting or violence and no recriminations. What more could a dog ask for? It sure beats suffering a lifetime of hard feelings for doing something it doesn't understand is wrong.

Lastly, take this bit of advice. Never correct or discipline a dog after you have called it to you or when it wanders over to you of its own accord. The canine mind makes direct, short-term connections. If your dog comes to you and you then discipline it, your dog will connect the correction with the act of coming to you (the most recent thing it did before the roof fell in) and *not* with what happened prior to that. After a few episodes of this, the dog will be reluctant to approach you, and eventually may not come at all. Therefore, if your dog has done something wrong beyond your immediate reach, either get up and go over to it for your correction or forget about it until you have the opportunity to do the job right in response to a future indiscretion.

©1980 — bryan hendrix

First Lessons

Long before you begin teaching your dog the five basic obedience commands, you'll need to accomplish several small "training" tasks. This includes housebreaking, of course, the first and most important lesson any dog must learn before it is an acceptable (and enduring) part of the family. Housebreaking is covered elsewhere in this book.

In addition, you should also begin to teach your puppy its name and how to walk on a leash during your first few weeks together. Dogs do not take naturally to the restraint of a leash, so you will have to slowly and steadily familiarize your puppy to accept a light lead.

It's also wise to establish good habits right from the start so you won't have to fuss with a lot of trouble-shooting later. This means keeping the puppy off the furniture, discouraging it from begging at the table (no table scraps!) and preventing chewing as well as other obnoxious practices. Let your puppy learn early what is acceptable and what is not.

Using a Training Collar and Lead

Serious obedience training should be postponed until a dog is approximately six to eight months old. Prior to that age, dogs have little power of concentration, and intense lessons will only confuse them. As a rule of thumb, puppies who are still teething are too young for earnest instruction.

Before you begin training your dog, purchase a training (choke) collar and lead (leash). A choke collar is usually composed of metal links, with a metal ring at each end. It forms a loop when the chain is slipped through one of the rings. The other ring is used for attaching the leash. The correct collar size may be determined by measuring around the largest part of the dog's head and then adding one inch. Training leads are made of leather or webbing, a half inch to a full inch wide, and measure six feet in length. Once you've got the right collar and lead, you should be ready to begin training.

The proper way to put on the choke collar is with the loose ring to the right of the dog's neck, the chain attached to it coming over the neck and through the holding ring, rather than under the neck. A collar in this orientation will work correctly, since the dog should stand at your left during training.

Before you start actually training the dog, give it time to adjust to the new collar by letting it wear it, always under supervision, for a day or so. Then snap the lead onto the collar and let the dog drag it around, watching that it doesn't get tangled. Once you feel the dog has accepted the collar and lead, take up your end and walk around for a while, applying little or no pressure. Then gradually, over a short period, increase your degree of control until the dog learns that even though the leash restrains it, there's no need to be afraid. Once you've reached the point where you can persuade your dog to come along in the general direction you want by gentle snaps on the lead, you are ready to begin obedience training.

Training collars are effective because you can exert as much or as little control as you need. You can command your dog's attention or urge it into the right position or direction by giving a *light, quick* snap on the lead. This momentarily tightens the collar around the neck. Just as quickly, pressure is then released from the lead and, if the collar is placed on the neck correctly, it will loosen instantly. Done properly, this process delivers a definite correction to the dog, which is really an attention getter—not an inducer of pain.

Some dogs need only a slight tug on the lead to relay the message. More recalcitrant dogs may require a greater show of strength. As training progresses, most dogs respond appropriately to only the slightest correction.

Never use the training collar to exert constant pressure on the dog's neck; despite its name, the collar is not meant for choking an animal into submission. A quick snap is all that should be required. In the right hands, training collars and leads are effective and humane tools. In the wrong hands, however, they can be harmful or even torturous.

Class Time

Training periods should take place regularly once or twice each day. Gradually increase the amount of time you spend training the dog from fifteen to thirty minutes. Longer sessions will not only tire the dog, but also tire the trainer, and overall training will suffer. Few things are worse for training than boredom, and that's exactly what is bound to happen when you try to pack too much learning into a session.

Be businesslike during training, but don't forget to be friendly (not frustrated) and offer lavish praise. At the completion of each lesson, take time to play freely with your dog, easing the pressure and communicating the idea that there will be time for fun as well as work.

Heeling

The heeling exercise forms the foundation for all the obedience lessons to follow. Teaching a dog to heel is vital if for no other reason than to be able to walk it properly. It's a drag—literally—to walk a dog who pulls you every which way. A dog who will not walk on lead is simply not a good companion, but rather a nuisance, if about the size of a breadbox, and a tyrant if commonly compared to a Mack truck. You shouldn't have to be a weight lifter to walk your dog and maintain control.

The following discussion about teaching a dog to heel will probably come across as highly disciplined and controlled. In the beginning, the process needs to be. Later, when the lesson is firmly ingrained, you can substitute a regular collar for the choke collar or attach the lead to both rings, preventing the application of additional pressure on the neck. At that stage, your dog should require only a vocal command to respond to your wishes.

To begin heeling, position the dog at your left side and start to walk while calling the dog's name and giving the command to heel: "Fido, heel!" A good training rule is to call the dog's name and then give the command for all movement exercises (heel, come) while giving only the command when you're teaching a motionless exercise (sit or stay).

Give the command just as you take the first step, and simultaneously lightly snap the lead to persuade the dog to move along. Remember also to step first with your left leg, the one closest to the dog if it's positioned correctly. (Another training rule:

step off with your right leg first if you're teaching a stationary exercise.)

Use only as much force as necessary to get the dog moving with you. As you walk along, continue to urge the dog to walk at your left side, with the neck and shoulder approximately opposite and level with your left leg, by snapping the lead. Each time, give the command "Heel!" as you snap. And each time you snap and command, follow it with praise. Be realistic; it will take a good deal of work before the dog understands what it is meant to do, for this is the first time it has ever been asked to perform on command. But if you are kind and patient and skillful, your dog will soon learn to do as asked—and without rancor, because it should realize that each time it responds properly, you are immensely pleased.

The secret of successful heeling training is learning the art of snapping the lead and hence tightening and releasing the choke collar. Remember that the less the choke is used to achieve the desired effect, and with the least amount of force, the better. You'll be using a series of quick jerks, not steady pressure, to make your message clear. And always offer praise with each jerk to remove the sting without removing the lesson.

Practice heeling in brief but lengthening sessions one or more times daily until you have to give only one command as you start walking and no longer need to use the lead for correction. Practice moving in circles, around corners and using other maneuvers, while keeping the dog at your side with continual snaps and praise, until you are confident that your dog is walking with you of its own accord. When heeling is well learned, you are ready to move on to teaching the sit. While you go over each new exercise, don't forget to incorporate past assignments into your regimen in order to keep the lessons fresh.

Sit

The sit command, in obedience training, means that the dog should sit at the handler's left side, the dog's shoulder square to the handler's knee. The dog should sit facing straight ahead. In fact, truly well-trained dogs learn to heel by their handler's side and then to automatically sit as soon as motion is stopped, such as when coming to a street corner.

Start by heeling the dog at your side. When you stop, give the command "Sit!" and place your left hand on the animal's rear to guide it into a sitting position while your right hand uses the lead to hold the head up. With hands positioned, make the dog remain sitting for a moment; then give the heel command and start walking once more. Again stop, give the command to sit, guide the dog into position and have it stay seated a little longer.

Gradually, as your dog catches on, you can quit giving the command, and then the lead and hand correction. The dog will sit automatically when you come to a stop, just as you've taught it to do, and wait for you to either start moving again or for its release through an established release command, such as "Okay!"

Finally, when your dog has learned the full meaning of sit, and learned to sit when you stop walking, you are ready to teach the sit from any position. Put the training collar and lead on, and give the dog the "Sit!" command, guiding it into position as before. Concentrate on this phase, continuing the pure sit training until your dog will sit on command without the need for corrections. When this is accomplished, you can begin to introduce the stay command.

Stay

Once your dog understands the command to stay, it should remain in a seated position until you release it. It doesn't matter if a cat passes by or a truckload of dog food jackknifes right in front of him. Your dog isn't completely trained unless its rear end maintains contact with the ground until the very moment you say it's okay to move.

To teach the stay, place your dog in a sitting position while on the lead. Tell it "Stay!", placing the palm of your left hand in front of the muzzle and taking one step away from the dog (start with your right foot; this is a stationary exercise). Repeat the "Stay!" command in a coaxing but firm voice and keep your hands on the dog, if necessary, to reinforce the command.

During the first few attempts, don't try to make your dog stay for more than ten or twenty seconds before releasing it. Slowly increase the time and the distance you step away while cutting down on the repeated vocal commands, until your dog will stay on one command for at least three minutes.

It is important for you to understand that the properly trained dog will do what it is told the *first and only* time it is told. During training, it's okay to give as many commands as it takes to get the idea across, but you must reach the point where you need to say only one "heel," "sit," or "stay" for the dog to respond. Once this is accomplished, you should deliver your single instruction in a firm but pleasant tone, and then use the lead and collar to ensure that your dog follows orders. Steer clear of the "rising voice syndrome." Most dogs aren't deaf and they certainly aren't insensitive; they are just improperly trained. Having to repeat your commands in tones of ever-increasing volume and frustration will not produce an obedient animal. You should meet with success if you remain firm and unequivocal.

Stand-Stay

Once your dog has mastered heeling and sitting, and sitting and staying, it is ready to learn the stand-stay. This is particularly useful during grooming sessions, for example.

The stand-stay is also taught from the heel. While the dog is heeling, slow to a halt and give the command, "Stand!" As you do so, stop the dog's forward motion with the lead and, before the animal has the chance to do the sit it has so wonderfully learned, block the forward and downward motion of its rear with your left hand, fingers extended, just in front of the top of its right hind leg. Don't grab the dog, just block it. If it still attempts to sit down, don't chastise, since it's only trying to do what you've already taught it. Simply start walking again with the "Heel!" command and after a few steps, stop again, using your left hand more firmly to prevent the dog from sitting.

The dog will probably be a little confused at this point, so use praise to reassure. While it is standing, give the "Stand!" command repeatedly, to let it know you want it to remain in that position, and also give the familiar "Stay!" command. Your dog should soon begin to understand.

Continue until your dog will stand firmly at your side when it hears the "Stand!" order, waiting for you to start heeling it again. If it tries to sit, simply start heeling again with the "Heel!" command. Combine this training with normal sits when you stop walking. If the dog is still unsure about what's going on, you may have to reinforce the sit with "Sit!" commands for a while. Soon it should become clear to the dog that it must sit unless there is a command to the contrary, and to stand when it hears the word.

Now you can begin to leave the dog alone briefly while either sitting or standing at the stay. Give a firm command to "Stay!" while simultaneously bringing your left hand around, fingers extended, to be held in front of the dog's nose with palm toward it. This is a signal to stay. With the leash still in your hand, step away from the dog, starting with the right foot. If the dog attempts to move or follow you, give a firm "No!" and then repeat the "Stay!" command, guiding it back into position with your hands and the lead.

If the dog seems confused once more, continue until it learns that it is now supposed to stay unless given a counter command to heel or is released. Step away again and move slowly until you are separated by the distance of the lead. Stay there for a few seconds before returning to praise the dog and release it. As training sessions continue, slowly increase the time you are away from the dog until you can stay away for at least a minute while it holds the stand position, and three minutes while it holds the sit. Once this is accomplished, you can begin to move around your dog while it is sitting or standing. Still holding the lead, walk away and circle around it, being careful that the lead neither tugs on it nor drags across the face. Continue until the dog will stay quietly and confidently for three minutes, while you walk away to the front, back or side and circle it several times without incident. Don't try to stop the dog from turning its head to watch you, but gently and firmly correct any break from position. Then reinforce it with the command again and leave once more.

Remember the necessity of praising your dog after every correction and whenever it does something right on its own initiative. At the risk of taxing your patience, we have not written, "Give praise," after each sentence in this section. It should appear in your mind nonetheless. There's no such thing as too much praise when you're training a dog, only too little.

Down

To teach your dog to lie down on command, sit it by your side. Kneel beside it and reach over its back with your left arm, taking hold of its upper left front leg; take hold of its right front leg similarly with your right hand. Tell the dog "Down!" and put it gently into the down position by lifting the front feet off the ground and easing the body down until the dog is in a lying position. This way, there is no struggle between the two of you. Your dog is comforted by the fact that your arm is held securely around it and will not feel the urge to struggle against the pressure of a leash or hand by bracing its front legs.

When the animal is down, release your grasp slowly, sliding your left hand around and leaving it on your dog's back. Keep saying "Down, stay!" as you do this. Make sure the dog remains in this position for a few seconds. Then release and command the dog into a sitting position for another try. Continue until your dog goes down at command without your having to lift it, and will stay quietly until released, without any pressure of your left hand on the back. Then give the command without putting your hands into the ready position. After a few days, you should be able to stand straight up and only give one command "Down!" for your dog to lie at your side. Your goal is then to improvise until it goes down when several feet away from you, still on lead.

When your dog has learned the down, leave it at the stay, as you did before with the sit and stand exercises. First walk away only briefly, and then leave for longer periods, finally circling around your dog. You will find this exercise easier than the earlier lesson, since the animal now knows the meaning of "Stay!"

Come

Perhaps the most important basic command a dog must learn is to respond immediately to "Come!" It comes last on our list of training exercises because your dog should first know how to respond to the other commands we've covered.

While your dog is heeling at your side, take a sudden step back and say, "Fido, come!" As you give the command, snap the lead to make the dog turn around to its right while walking, and get it headed back toward you. When your dog is facing you, keep walking backward, urging it to come toward you with continued gentle snaps of the lead and repetitions of the "Come!" command.

Offering praise is especially important here, since this is a puzzling turn of events for your dog. When it is in full stride toward you, stop, and give the command "Sit!" as it reaches you. It may be necessary to guide the dog into a sitting position directly in front of you, but there is a good chance you won't need to. Once it is in position directly in front of and facing you, the first "recall" is completed. Tell the dog "Stay!" and walk around into position, then start up at heel again for another try.

Continue working this way until you have only to step backward and give the command, with no lead, urging the dog to turn and walk to you and then sit in front of you without further command. From here, the progression to the recall from a sitting position at a distance should be simple. Get the dog to sit, then step away to the end of the lead. Then give the "Come!" command. If your dog hesitates, give slight snap on the lead to let it know what you want, and the animal should get up, come to you and sit in front.

Notice that there is never a tug of war going on between you and your dog in teaching this command. Your dog is already in motion when you give the "Come!" while heeling, so you don't have to struggle with the lead to get the dog out of a stationary position.

English Setters. *Julie Ward*

A beautiful, well-trained dog is a source of deep, lasting satisfaction. It is also the way to enter an exciting world of active competition, lifelong friendships and a kind of pleasure that must be experienced to be fully appreciated.

·6·

COMPETITIONS FOR YOU AND YOUR DOG

ONCE YOUR DOG UNDERSTANDS the six basic commands, you're ready for the final step: obedience without the control of the lead. This is known as off-lead work. In preparation, you must be absolutely certain that your dog will obey commands without hesitation while on lead. This is a common place for training to break down. Many home trainers do not adequately train their dogs to the point where responses are reliable with a lead, but they go ahead and try off-lead work, anyway. The outcome is invariably fatal to the training.

Assuming you and your dog have progressed successfully to this point, seat the dog at your side as before. Take the lead off and start with the heel command. You will probably be greatly surprised (and thrilled!) to find that your dog heels with you. It shouldn't be a surprise, though, if your previous training has been consistent and thorough. Go through the whole routine: the stands, downs, sits and stays, just as if the lead were still there. Before you do the recall, however, be warned. Don't start trying it at distances of more than six feet. You must slowly work up to greater distances. As with most things in training, gradual progress is the norm.

In most cases, if all has gone well before, all will go well now.

If not, put the lead back on for corrections whenever necessary. Work on those shaky parts until the dog performs them properly and then remove the lead and try again. It should work.

Everyone can have a well-trained dog if he is patient and applies the methods we have outlined here. The key is to be consistent and persistent. Of course, confidence is the most important ingredient in good training: confidence in yourself as a trainer and in your dog as an intelligent, receptive student. We're already assuming that you have earned your dog's respect and that you are a kind, fair and firm owner. Training is not accomplished in a day, a week or even a month, so be patient. Accomplishing your goal, however, can be fun—not a chore—if you go about it right. The result will be a dog that responds to your wishes, a joy to own and a true companion.

Canine Good Citizens

The American Kennel Club sponsors a program administered by dog clubs throughout the United States to encourage all dog owners to train their dogs. The program is called the Canine Good Citizen.

In it, dog owners have their dogs evaluated on a pass/fail basis for ten different activities that a good canine citizen would be expected to be capable of performing. Dogs who pass are awarded a Canine Good Citizen Certificate.

Included are such things as allowing a stranger to approach, walking naturally on a loose lead, walking through a crowd, sitting for examination, reacting to a strange dog and reacting to a distraction such as a door suddenly closing or a jogger running by the dog.

When you've got your boisterous pup in shape you might want to try a Canine Good Citizen test. Look for notices in your local paper or contact the AKC for the name of the club nearest you that sponsors these evaluations. And for those of you who would like to try actual Obedience competition, there are thousands of Obedience Trials held each year by AKC clubs. More about Obedience competition can be found on pages 118–120.

The Sport of Showing Dogs

Showing dogs is no longer an activity enjoyed only by the very wealthy. Today's competitors come from all parts of the country and from all segments of society. Some people choose to show their own dogs; others hire professional handlers whose expertise is exhibiting dogs to their best advantage.

The sport of showing dogs usually confounds most newcomers. The participants, the rules, even the outcome of the judging are difficult to decipher at first. In this section, you'll find a basic explanation of the dog show process. If you then attend a few dog shows to observe the process in action—and sample the infectious appeal of seeing beautiful animals compete against one another for top honors—you, too, may join the growing number of dog show devotees.

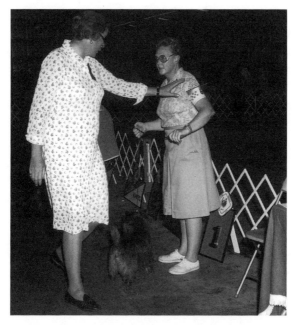

Showing dogs is one of America's most popular participant sports and it keeps right on growing. In conformation competition, dogs are shown against one another and compared to their breed Standard by the judge in order to select the winners. Many rules govern the conduct of dog shows, but the attraction of the game is meeting the challenge of competition and coming up with the winner. The veteran exhibitor would have it no other way.

The Competition

Each year, more than 10,000 competitive events are held under American Kennel Club rules. There are six types of competition: dog shows, field trials, hunting trials, tracking tests, Obedience Trials, and herding. In each of these categories, there are formal licensed events (point shows at which championship points or credit toward field or Obedience titles may be earned) and informal events (match shows at which no points or credits are earned).

Dog Shows

The majority of the competitive events held under AKC rules are *dog shows*, where the emphasis lies on *conformation*. After examining the entry, each judge decides how close, in his or her opinion, the dogs measure up to that judge's mental image of the perfect dog as described in the breed Standard. The dogs are also compared to one another. Ultimately, the judge places the best dogs in each regular class from first to fourth.

Most dogs seen at shows are competing for points toward their championships. It takes fifteen points to become a Champion of Record, which then entitles the owner to use "Ch." before the dog's name. Essentially, these points are based upon the number of dogs in actual competition—the more dogs, the more points. However, the number of dogs required for points varies with the breed, the sex and the geographical location of the show in accordance with a schedule annually designated by the AKC to help equalize competition from breed to breed and area to area.

A dog can earn from one to five points at a show. Wins of three, four or five points are termed "majors." The fifteen points required for championship must be won under at least three different judges, and must include two majors won under different judges.

Dogs compete in five or more regular classes to earn their points. These five classes are the Puppy (which may be divided by age), Novice, Bred-by-Exhibitor, American-bred and Open (which may also be divided for a number of reasons). The class in which the dog is entered depends, among other things, on its age and previous wins.

Only one male and one female of each breed can win points at each show. Only males compete against males, and females against females in the classes for points.

Judging in every breed is the same. The judge begins with the Puppy class. In each class the dogs are evaluated and the top four in the judge's opinion are placed first through fourth. However, only the first place winner in each class remains in competition; the others are eliminated.

After the judge has made his or her decisions in the regular classes, the winners from each class are brought back to compete against each other. This is called the Winners Class. The dog selected best is the Winners Dog. He is the male who receives the points at the show.

Following selection of the Winners Dog, the dog that placed second to him in his original class of competition is brought into the ring to compete with the other class winners for Reserve Winners Dog. The Reserve will receive the points if for any reason the Winners win is disallowed by the AKC.

The same process is repeated for bitches, with a Winners Bitch (the only female of the breed to receive points at the show) and a Reserve Winners Bitch being selected.

The judge must now evaluate one more class in the breed and make three more awards. The Best of Breed class includes all the Champions of Record competing, male and female, and the Winners Dog and Winners Bitch. The judge goes over all the dogs and selects one Best of Breed. Then, between the Winners Dog and Winners Bitch, the judge selects a Best of Winners. If either the Winners Dog or Winners Bitch is selected Best of Breed, it automatically becomes Best of Winners. The judge then finishes the breed judging by selecting a Best of Opposite Sex to the Best of Breed.

At an all-breed show, this process of elimination takes place in all the breeds represented. Then, each Best of Breed winner competes for first place within its Group. Four placements are awarded in each Group, but only the first is eligible to compete

To the dog exhibitor, every new puppy is a new beginning and every promising puppy generates the hope of winning days ahead. The beautiful new puppy also means training, grooming and long hours of work, but it's worth everything when the puppy you banked on justifies your faith. There are sessions where the puppy will learn to allow itself to be handled: to have its mouth closely examined, to gait in a straight line on a loose lead, and to have its rear parts handled without protesting. These are the early lessons for every potential show dog.

English Setter. *Beresford Photos*

in the final competition. This whittles the competition down to seven individuals vying for Best in Show. At the largest all-breed events, nearly 4000 contestants are evaluated before one dog is awarded the Best in Show ribbon.

Confused? This may all be a little overwhelming at first, like learning a new language. Rest assured that it becomes much clearer once you've sat through the actual process a few times. The other bonus of attending dog shows is the chance to mingle with a large crowd of enthusiastic experts, just waiting to interpret the proceedings as they unfold. Ask away.

Obedience Trials

Obedience Trials test a dog's ability to perform a prescribed set of exercises. The performance for each exercise is scored by a judge. You might consider Obedience a competition of handler and dog. Conformation has no bearing on the dog's ability to compete in Obedience; individuals that would be disqualified from the show ring, such as neutered animals, may compete for an Obedience title.

Obedience is divided into three levels, each more difficult than its predecessor. At each level, competitors work for an AKC Obedience degree or title.

The first level is called Novice. The Novice exercises include those things all dogs should be taught to make them good companions. These include heeling, standing for examination, coming when called and staying on command. Successful competitors earn the title of Companion Dog (CD).

Labrador Retrievers, German Shepherd Dog. *Mary Bloom*

Obedience training and trials give dogs one of their most positive profiles. Introduced in America in the early 1930s, this sport is avidly followed by owners of all breeds and is as exciting for the spectator as for the competitor. Obedience is not like conformation in format but, like conformation, it requires lots of behind-the-scenes fine tuning and practice.

Open work is next. It introduces seven exercises such as retrieving a dumbbell, jumping a hurdle and broad jumping. If a dog completes an Open title, it is called a Companion Dog Excellent (CDX).

The third, and most advanced, level is known as Utility. Scent discrimination and responding to hand signals are among the exercises included at this level. The title earned by dogs mastering this work is Utility Dog (UD). Only dogs that have earned the Utility Dog title can earn points toward an Obedience Trial Championship (OTCH), the ultimate distinction.

To receive an Obedience title, a dog must earn three "legs." To get credit for a leg, a dog must score at least 170 points out of a possible 200, and earn more than 50 percent on each exercise. The passing score and grand total are the same at each level, even though the exercises vary in complexity.

Tracking Tests

Tracking tests, held under AKC regulations, require a dog to follow a trail by scent. A dog passing such a test earns a Tracking Dog title (TD). Mastery of a more advanced test entitles a dog to use the letters TDX for Tracking Dog Excellent after its name.

Field Trials and Hunting Tests

Field trials are held separately for pointing breeds, retrievers and spaniels, as well as Beagles, Basset Hounds and Dachshunds. Field trials are practical demonstrations of the dog's ability to perform, in the field, the functions for which they were bred. The titles that are awarded are Field Champion and Amateur Field Champion.

Retrievers, pointing breeds and spaniels are also eligible to participate in Hunting tests. Here, owners of these breeds can obtain an evaluation of their dogs' hunting ability. A dog's performance is evaluated at three levels, and again, each succeeding level is increasingly difficult. Dogs successfully completing the respective levels earn the titles Junior Hunter, Senior Hunter and Master Hunter.

Herding

The herding program is divided into Testing and Trial sections.

In the Testing section, dogs can earn the titles of Herding Test Dog (HT) and Pre-Trial Tested Dog (PT). The former is awarded to dogs that show an inherent herding ability and are trainable in herding. The PT title, on the other hand, is earned by dogs with some training in herding, and can, therefore, herd a small group of livestock through a simple course.

German Shorthaired Pointer.   *Linda Nickerson*

Field trials for pointing breeds, retrievers and spaniels, along with events for Beagles, Basset Hounds and Dachshunds, enjoy a large, enthusiastic following in the United States. These events serve to keep the breed's aptitude for their original work sharp while providing exciting recreation for large numbers of people.

Pembroke Welsh Corgi. *Callea*

Herding tests and trials are a fairly recent addition to the events in which dogs can distinguish themselves. It is truly amazing how many dogs of the herding breeds demonstrate their proficiency even if they have never been in the presence of livestock.

Trials offer four titles, beginning with the Herding Started (HS), Herding Intermediate (HI), and Herding Excellent (HX) titles. After earning an HX, dogs can then accumulate the necessary fifteen championship points for the Herding Championship (HCH). Such a dog is proficient in herding and capable of controlling even the most difficult livestock in diverse situations. The trials are run on three distinct courses, which differ in both physical appearance and style of herding.

Whatever your interest and wherever you live, it shouldn't be difficult to locate an AKC event in your area. A list of up-coming shows and trials is included with each issue of the AKC's monthly magazine, *Purebred Dogs/American Kennel Gazette*. Many clubs advertise their events in local newspapers as well.

Junior Showmanship

If there are youngsters between the ages of ten and eighteen in your family, an entire class of competition exists to help them develop handling skills. Called Junior Showmanship, this competition is judged solely on the ability and skills of the handler—not on the dog's actual conformation. Junior Showmanship is a great place to learn skillful dog handling for conformation competition. It's also a terrific way to make new acquaintances with other young people who share an interest in showing dogs.

Adults, unfortunately, do not have an equivalent of Junior Showmanship. However, novice handlers may find a local match, where no points are awarded, a good place to start. Just remember—no dog becomes a champion overnight. It takes plenty of hard work before, during and even after each show. Often, a lot of traveling is required before a dog earns enough points for its title. But few people will deny the thrill they get from introducing their dog as an American Kennel Club Champion of Record!

Saint Bernards. *Marianne Peters*

To a dedicated breeder, consistency of type in his or her dogs is a great satisfaction. Always remember, though, that breeding dogs should never be undertaken lightly or for the wrong reasons. If you plan to breed your dog, you must assume responsibility for the health and safety of the mother and puppies. Otherwise, if you don't plan to show, have your dog neutered. You won't be sorry.

·7·

BREEDING

YOU MAY EVENTUALLY DECIDE to breed your dog. In that case, the following discussion of canine reproduction will not seem premature—even if your own puppy has yet to be chosen. Allow us a moment to preach, however. Please don't take this responsibility lightly. There are already far too many unwanted dogs in the world. As dog lovers, let's try to resolve rather than aggravate this unfortunate situation. You must have plans for each and every puppy before the litter is even conceived.

Also, it's over-optimistic to assume that you can recoup your investment or even profit by breeding dogs. Few people come out ahead by selling puppies, once they have paid stud fees, provided veterinary care and food for the mother and litter and have accounted for their enormous investment of time.

Breeding dogs also has its emotional costs. Ask a breeder what it's like to see a bitch through a difficult birth or Caesarean section, or to witness the death of a beloved bitch or her puppies. Death plays as large a role as life when it comes to breeding dogs, and rare is the litter in which all the puppies survive.

But while you're at it, ask about the excitement and challenge of breeding dogs. Catch a glimpse of how it feels to be responsible for building a solid foundation for future generations of dogs. This will really help make up your mind whether breeding dogs is right for you.

And if you decide to go forward and become a breeder, we hope you will embrace the belief that each new litter you produce should represent an improvement over the last. This means that you don't choose the dog who lives down the street to mix genes with your bitch because he happens to be close by and performs for free. Try to find an individual whose bloodlines will strengthen your dog's weaknesses and emphasize his or her good qualities. The rewards of your discretion will be long-lived.

Selecting Breeding Partners

It is not our purpose here to delve into the genetics of breeding better dogs. There are many excellent books entirely devoted to the genetics of the dog and how to breed. There are three important points we wish to make, however, concerning the selection of a breeding partner for your dog.

First, as complicated as genetics may seem, there is a simple principle to bear in mind in selecting dogs; namely, you mate animals that complement one another. Meaning, for example, if your dog's coat is not as good as it might be, then locate a partner with a good coat from a line with good coats. The truth is, of course, that selecting breeding partners is more complex, because you must weigh all the factors that make up the two animals. Obviously, this is one area where experienced breeders are your absolute best resource.

The second and third points we want you to digest boil down to two words: *temperament* and *health*. Temperament is a hereditary trait in dogs. Selection over many generations eventually produced breeds with the correct temperament to pull sleds, follow scent on trails or retrieve game. The inheritance factors of temperament are complex. However, never consider breeding a dog with questionable temperament. You impose a major disservice on both human and canine communities if you produce another generation of skittish or bad-tempered animals.

In addition, dogs are subject to many hereditary defects, some of which are potentially crippling or fatal. If you breed, you carry the responsibility of ensuring that the dogs you produce

Correct temperament is one of the breeder's most pressing priorities. Even though most dogs will never see the inside of a show ring, the way they respond and relate to people is directly tied to how well they conform to the Standard. A fancier may choose to tolerate bad temperament in a beautiful dog, but the person who wants a good companion dog should never be forced to make that choice. *Ralph G. Thompson*

are not affected by the major known hereditary diseases occurring in your breed. Both your dog's breeder and your veterinarian can advise you. Please do not take this warning lightly. Consider how devastated you would feel if the beautiful eight-week-old puppy you place in a loving home develops a crippling hip problem at one year of age. Ignorance is no excuse for having contributed to this tragic situation.

Reproductive Physiology

The age at which dogs reach sexual maturity depends to a large extent on their breed. Small breeds tend to mature faster than

The breeder must do everything possible to keep his or her stock free of hereditary defects. Only known breeding records can isolate the sources of many defects and diseases. Without a knowledge of the breeding history of a specific family, it is virtually impossible to say whether or not a young puppy will experience devastating health problems as an adult. *Carol Hunter*

large breeds. In general, male puppies become fertile after six months of age and reach full fertility by twelve to fifteen months. Healthy stud dogs may remain sexually active and fertile up to eight to ten years old or older. Adult males are able to mate at any time.

Bitches experience their first estrus (also known as season and heat) sometime after six months of age, although a wide variation occurs, with eighteen months not uncommon in some larger breeds. Estrus recurs at intervals of six to seven months on the average, depending on the breed and individual, until late in life. During the estrus period, the female is fertile and will accept the male.

The reproductive cycle of the bitch is divided into four stages:

1. *Proestrus* This is the time when males are attracted to females. A bloody vaginal discharge is observed, as well as distinct swelling of the external genitalia. Proestrus lasts approximately nine days; the female, however, will not allow mating at this stage.
2. *Estrus* Estrus also lasts approximately nine days. During this phase, females will allow males to mount. Ovulation usually occurs in the first forty-eight hours; however, this is extremely variable. Fertilization can take place during estrus if the bitch is inseminated by a fertile dog.
3. *Diestrus* The third stage, lasting sixty to ninety days, occurs when the reproductive tract is under the control of progesterone. This happens whether or not the bitch becomes pregnant. False pregnancy, a condition in which the bitch shows all the symptoms of being pregnant although she has not conceived, is occasionally seen during diestrus.
4. *Anestrus* This is the period following diestrus when no sexual activity takes place. It lasts for three to four months.

Breeding

There are many schools of thought regarding when to begin breeding a bitch. It is customary, however, not to breed at the first heat to avoid imposing the stress of pregnancy and lactation on a young, growing animal. Another common practice is to avoid breeding a bitch on consecutive heats, to allow sufficient time for recuperation between pregnancies. If breeding on the first heat or on consecutive heats occurs, extra attention and care are mandatory to reduce the risk of potential problems. Ask your veterinarian for advice on this subject.

At least one month prior to breeding, the bitch should be in good condition. This means most emphatically that she is not overweight, and is in good muscle tone. She should have a thorough prebreeding physical examination by a veterinarian. Her vaccinations should be current, and she should be tested and treated for parasites. You may wish to have her tested for brucellosis, a bacterial disease that can cause sterility or spon-

taneous abortion in affected dogs. (Ask the owner of the stud dog if he's had his dog tested for brucellosis, since a male carrier can infect the female. If he is used for breeding frequently, a test before each mating is probably impractical. In that case, it is usually acceptable for the dog to be kept away from pregnant, whelping and nursing bitches, and to be tested twice yearly.)

Breeding management varies widely from breed to breed. Most commonly, the breeding takes place between the tenth and fourteenth day after the onset of proestrus. The signs of estrus are obvious in some bitches, but others benefit from having vaginal smears analyzed by a veterinarian to identify the fertile period. While the bitch will stand for the male, mating every other day for a total of two or three times is considered good breeding management for most dogs.

Females are usually less inhibited by new environments, so bitches are commonly taken to the stud. The first time a young male is used, breeding will proceed more smoothly if an experienced bitch is used. Nevertheless, sometimes breeding must be assisted by human handlers, to provide support or guidance. Some breeds are more apt to need assistance than others because of anatomical considerations. This is another area that should be discussed with your own dog's breeder prior to the big event.

During breeding, the male will mount the female from the rear and clasp her middle with his front legs. He will then rapidly thrust his pelvis until he penetrates the bitch and ejaculation takes place. After his pelvic thrusts cease, the dogs remain locked together by a normal swelling that takes place in the male's penis. This is commonly called a tie, and may be expected to last from ten to thirty minutes. Do not try to separate the dogs during the tie, because it can injure them. The male may turn around while he and the female are joined, so that they stand rear to rear. At the end of the tie, the dogs will separate naturally.

Artificial insemination in dogs is approved by the American Kennel Club. For complete details about AKC policies contact Registration Service, 5580 Centerview Drive, Raleigh, NC, 27606.

Pregnancy

A normal canine pregnancy lasts approximately sixty-three days following conception. Signs of pregnancy include increased appetite, weight and breast size. Bitches with false pregnancy can also exhibit these symptoms, however. Veterinarians can usually diagnose pregnancy through abdominal palpation at twenty-eight days or by using ultrasound or X-ray tests.

Once pregnancy is confirmed, it's time to review special feeding requirements and what to expect before, during and after the birth with your veterinarian. You should also be briefed on how to recognize and respond to an emergency.

A few days before she gives birth (known as whelping), the bitch may refuse to eat and start to build her nest, where she plans to have her puppies. Unless you introduce her beforehand to a whelping box, the delivery room may be your closet, the

space under your bed or any number of places you would probably consider inappropriate.

A whelping box should be sufficiently large to accommodate a comfortable stretch for the bitch. It should have low sides and be placed in a warm, dry, draft-free and secluded place. Place towels or other soft material in the bottom of the whelping box. Fresh newspapers are also fine and may be easily removed and replaced as they become soiled during whelping. Once whelping is completed, however, you should replace the newspapers with something that provides better footing for the puppies.

Shortly before whelping, the bitch's body temperature will drop to 99 degrees or lower (normal temperature for a dog is between 100 and 102.5 degrees). By this time, you should have shaved her belly, where appropriate, to allow the puppies to find the nipples. If she has a long or dense coat, you should also shave and clean the area around her genitals.

Approximately twenty-four hours after her temperature drops, she can be expected to enter the first stage of labor, when the cervix dilates and opens the birth canal for the passage of puppies. At this time, she will pant, strain, appear restless or may perhaps vomit. Vomiting is normal at the onset of labor, but persistent vomiting may be a sign of illness. This stage of labor is followed by actual abdominal straining and production of the puppies and placentas.

Birth

Most bitches give birth easily, without the need of human help. Each puppy emerges in its own placental membrane, which must be removed before the puppy can breathe. The mother usually takes care of this by tearing off and eating the membrane, and then severs the umbilical cord. After delivery, she will lick each puppy to stimulate its breathing. Frequent licking, which continues for three weeks or so, also has another vital function: it stimulates the puppy to excrete waste. Without maternal assistance puppies cannot do so. At the time of birth, new mothers are also busy cleaning their offspring, warming them and allowing them to suckle. It is very important for the puppies to suckle soon after emerging from the womb. Suckling lets them ingest colostrum, a milklike substance containing maternal antibodies which is produced in the mammary glands just after birth. Colostrum helps the newborn puppies fight infection in their early days, while their own immune systems mature.

A placenta follows each puppy after a few minutes and is generally eaten by the mother. Try to keep track of the number of placentas delivered to make sure one is produced for each puppy. A retained placenta may cause infection.

Occasionally, a bitch neglects to remove a placental membrane or sever an umbilical cord, or she may be unable to do the job herself. In that case, you must handle the situation without delay. Puppies can remain inside the placental sac after birth for only a few minutes before the oxygen supply is depleted. Remove the puppy from the sac by tearing the membrane first from the face and head and then working backward. Then clean any mucus or fluid from the puppy's mouth and nose, and stimulate its circulation by rubbing it briskly with a towel. Tie off the umbilical cord with unwaxed dental floss, and cut the cord about two inches from the abdomen. Apply iodine to the cut end to prevent a navel infection.

When to Call the Veterinarian

If events during delivery take an ominous turn, don't hesitate to call the veterinarian for assistance. Abnormal conditions that signify trouble include:

1. indications of extreme pain
2. straining in labor for over three hours without passing a puppy, whether one or no puppies have been delivered previously
3. trembling, shivering or collapse
4. passage of a dark green or bloody fluid before the birth of the first puppy (after the first puppy, this is normal).

Also, veterinarians commonly recommend that you schedule a health check for the bitch and her puppies within a day of the delivery.

Newborn Puppies

Newborn puppies are unable to control their body temperature. They must be kept in a place where the temperature is approximately 85 degrees Fahrenheit. Chilling during these early days of life causes stress and predisposes the puppies to infectious disease. The puppies' environment may be kept warm by using a well-insulated heating pad (preferably one which uses circulating warm water), an electric heating bulb or a hot water bottle covered with a towel for protection.

Sometimes a bitch is unable or unwilling to care for her puppies. When that happens, it's up to you to feed the puppies, stimulate them and keep them warm.

Cow's milk is a poor substitute for bitch's milk, which is more concentrated, has twice the level of protein, almost double the

Blind, deaf and helpless, the newborn puppy must have many critical needs met in order to survive. If you were suddenly left with the responsibility of a newborn litter whose mother would not care for them, would you be able to handle it? *Dennis Bond*

Under normal circumstances a healthy bitch is very capable of caring for her litter and raising her puppies to weaning age. Care must be taken to keep the puppies away from drafts because their chilling effects can be lethal to newborns. *Furman*

caloric content and more than twice the content of calcium and phosphorus. Your best bet is to buy a complete puppy formula and enough pet nursing bottles with nipples for your entire litter at a local pet store or veterinary hospital.

Tilt the bottle to prevent the puppy from ingesting air. Don't let it nurse too rapidly. The hole in the nipple should be just large enough to let milk ooze slowly out when the bottle is inverted. Refer to the directions on the product to determine the quantity and frequency you need to feed. To be on the safe side,

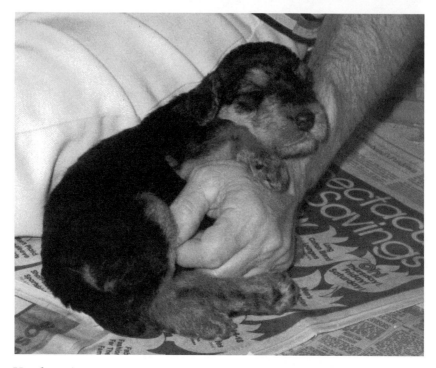

Hand-rearing one or more puppies can be a tremendous task and the chance of losing some of a litter is very great. Even though hand-reared puppies are usually very people oriented, most breeders would leave the early care of puppies to their mothers whenever possible. *Frances Sikorski*

however, if you need to resort to these measures, you should be following a veterinarian's orders. He or she can guide you through the correct procedure and teach you how to tube feed the puppies, if necessary.

The puppies will need stimulation to urinate and defecate after each feeding. This is accomplished by gently massaging the anal region with a moistened cotton ball.

Hand rearing puppies is extremely time-consuming and not without its difficulties. Ready yourself for the probable loss of some members of the litter. A bitch who stubbornly refuses to care for her young probably shouldn't be bred again unless you're ready to assume full responsibility for more puppies in the future.

Weaning the Puppies

Most puppies begin the weaning process at about three weeks of age. You can start them off by offering a pan of formula in place of their mother's milk. Next, replace the formula with a combination of pablum and formula. Hand-fed puppies may be removed from the bottle at this time, and meat or high quality canned dog food may be offered in addition to the pablum/ formula mixture. At five weeks, delete pablum from the gruel and replace the formula with a solution of equal parts of evaporated milk and water. In addition to the meat and canned food, a good commercial dry or moist dog food can be introduced into the feeding program.

All changes in food or feeding schedules should be made gradually to allow the digestive system time to adjust. A sudden change often leads to diarrhea.

The preceding discussion has barely touched the surface of the basics about breeding and raising a litter to weaning. If you are considering breeding, we advise you to do as much preparation and study as possible. This includes researching the subject and talking with experienced breeders as well as your veterinarian. A good reason to investigate your local dog clubs is to find experienced breeders who can offer good advice and guidance.

Weaning usually begins at about three weeks, and most often, puppies learn to eat from a communal food pan. At first, weanlings make an incredible mess of themselves, but by the time they reach the maturity level of these Smooth Dachshunds, they become very skilled at handling mealtimes. *William Lavendar*

·8·

ILLNESS: SIGNS AND SYMPTOMS

Every living thing gets sick at some point in its life, dogs included; it's unfair to expect otherwise. But if you've been careful, and chosen a healthy puppy right from the start, you've built a solid foundation to grow on.

Good preventative care gives your dog as much protection against illness as possible. It grants the dog strength to fight infection, keeps it free from debilitating parasites and, through regular vaccinations, gives immunity against potentially fatal diseases like distemper and parvovirus. Yearly checkups, which are usually performed when booster shots are given, should not be neglected since they can detect problems before they become obvious.

But illness can strike any dog at any time. Get to know your dog's normal actions and responses, so something out of the ordinary immediately attracts your attention. And remember that you must act as your dog's interpreter to communicate what's wrong, so be alert and observant at all times.

If your dog exhibits any of the following signs, a visit to the veterinarian is warranted.

1. loss of appetite or ravenous appetite without weight gain
2. increased thirst and/or frequency of urination
3. diarrhea or constipation
4. vomiting or gagging

5. discharge from the eyes, nose or mouth
6. coughing or respiratory difficulty
7. straining to urinate or the production of abnormal urine
8. pain, shivering or fever
9. unexplained restlessness or weight loss
10. problems with walking or moving

Add to the list anything about your dog that is out of the ordinary *for it*. You are the best judge of what's normal and what's not.

The following section describes a select few canine illnesses commonly seen by veterinarians. Each is grouped according to the general area affected and is characterized by common symptoms.

But first, a few more words of warning. *Time* is often the deciding factor in the ability to diagnose and treat an illness. Therefore, we urge you to use this section as a resource in getting to know the canine species—*not* as a guide to diagnosing your own dog. Diseases don't always "read the book" and show up exactly as expected. Let a veterinarian use his or her professional judgment to diagnose and treat the problem—and the sooner the better.

The Skin

The skin is the largest organ of the dog's body and a frequent source of problems. The job of the skin is to protect the inner organs and tissues from invasions by foreign substances, changing temperature and dehydration. The skin also works to synthesize essential vitamins for the rest of the body and performs the indispensable job of processing information about the external world through sensation.

Normal canine skin is smooth and flexible. Colors range from pale pink to brown to bluish black. Spotted skin is normal in any dog, even those whose coats are uniform in color. Lumps, bumps, scabs, scales, patches of hair loss or parasites shouldn't be visible anywhere on a healthy dog's body.

Dogs have seasonal shedding cycles, which don't always behave according to strict schedule. There are so many different kinds of canine hair that it's difficult to draw a typical picture. Obviously the hair of a Miniature Schnauzer shouldn't grow in like that of a Golden Retriever! Perhaps it's best to concentrate on what hair shouldn't be. It shouldn't break or pull out easily, or seem excessively dry or oily. In a smooth-coated dog, the coat should not appear dull or weak. Any sudden or significant change in the hair's appearance should be brought to the attention of your veterinarian.

External Parasites

Fleas. Fleas are tiny wingless insects that feed on dogs, among other animals. Flea bites make some dogs, who are allergic to the flea saliva, so miserable that they bite and scratch themselves raw. Other dogs do not seem to respond to flea bites with the same intensity. No matter. If you see evidence of fleas on your dog, it is essential to eradicate them as quickly as possible, before their population grows. Hungry fleas sometimes bite humans, too, leaving small, red, itchy bumps most commonly observed on the wrists and ankles.

How can you tell if your dog has fleas? You may actually see the dark fleas, about the size of sesame seeds, scurrying about on the skin. Their favorite haunts include the base of the ears and the rump. Look closely in sparsely haired places like the groin for telltale signs. A more accurate way to diagnose fleas, however, when live ones aren't observed, is to part the fur in several places and look for tiny black specks about the size of poppy seeds. These specks are flea feces, composed of digested blood. If you're not sure whether you're looking at "flea dirt" or just plain dirt, place it on a damp piece of white tissue. After a minute or so, a small red spot or halo will become apparent if it's flea feces, since the blood rehydrates and diffuses into the tissue.

The flea comb is a handy item which helps you determine if your dog has fleas. The teeth are set very close together and snare flea evidence when the comb is drawn through the dog's

©1982-bryan hendrix

coat. If you trap a flea, crush it immediately. Though wingless, fleas can jump so fast and so far that they practically disappear the second you see them.

Getting rid of fleas entails killing them on the dog as well as in the environment. For this, you may need an armament of products best purchased from a veterinarian.

Undoubtedly the most popular flea product people purchase for their dogs is the flea collar. Flea collars are impregnated with a chemical intended to kill and repel fleas. They work for a limited period, depending on the type you buy and the conditions it is subjected to.

The flea collar is your first step in dealing with fleas. Don't let it end there. While this product will probably reduce the amount of fleas on your dog, its use alone will not lead to a flea-free animal. You must combine flea collars with other forms of protection.

©1980 — bryan hendrix

A flea shampoo kills fleas on the animal, but usually leaves no residual protection against future fleas. For this purpose, you need either a dip (applied to the dog after its bath and allowed to dry right on the coat) or a flea spray or powder. Talk to your veterinarian about which product is recommended for your dog, depending on age and condition. Read and follow the exact instructions on each product before use.

As for your home, flea bombs set off in each room or living area is an effective way to kill fleas. Premise sprays can also be applied throughout the house. Thorough vacuuming before home treatment is recommended; discard the vacuum cleaner bag once this job is finished. It is important to treat all areas where the dog has traveled, since flea eggs may be present on the floor or furniture. In desperate situations, a yard or kennel spray may be necessary to kill outside fleas.

You must understand that just killing fleas on your dog is not enough to prevent the infestation from repeating itself. The environment must also be treated, as well as any other dogs or cats that live in the household. Also, flea eggs may survive for several weeks after live adults have been eliminated. Repeat treatments may be necessary.

Fortunately, in many parts of the United States, freezing weather goes a long way toward putting an end to outside fleas. In temperate areas, the flea battle may rage year-round. Sometimes it's best to consult a professional exterminator if the infestation in your house is severe.

Ticks. Ticks are a problem throughout the country, especially in rural and beach areas. This parasite is most widely known for its association with Lyme disease in people and animals. It can also cause anemia, tick paralysis or other serious blood-borne diseases in the dog. Ticks should be removed as soon as they are discovered, and then destroyed. Make a habit of checking your dog's entire body for ticks, especially the face, ears, feet and underside. If you are concerned about Lyme disease, bring any ticks you find (bottled, please) to a veterinarian for identification; not all ticks are known vectors for the disease.

The correct way to remove a tick is to grasp it as close to the skin as possible with a pair of tweezers or hemostats and then pull the tick straight out. Don't touch the tick with your fingers. There's no need to soak the tick first with any chemical products.

Don't be too concerned if you leave a tiny piece of the tick in the skin. It will not grow back and usually does not cause infection. You may notice a small red bump in the area as the skin reacts to the site of attachment. Clean the area daily with hydrogen peroxide and check it for further problems, in which case see the veterinarian.

Most flea sprays, powders and dips also protect against tick infestation. Still, in light of the seriousness of disease to both human and canine, regular inspection for ticks is well advised, especially in warm weather in areas where ticks are known to be a problem.

Lice. Fortunately, lice infestations are relatively uncommon in the dog. Spread by direct contact with an affected animal, these parasites cause intense itching. Lice appear as tiny, pale-colored creatures on the surface of the skin. They are easily eradicated with the proper medicated bath, dip or other product prescribed by a veterinarian.

Mites. Mites are microscopic parasites that inhabit the surface or follicles of the skin. Depending on the type, they can cause mild, moderate or intense misery. On the other hand, no signs at all may be observed.

For instance, one of the most common types of mite infestations of the dog, demodectic mange, causes unsightly skin lesions but ordinarily arouses no response in affected dogs. Usually a problem of young dogs, demodectic mange is suspected when patches of redness and hair loss appear on the forehead, eyes, muzzle and forepaws. Some dogs outgrow their mange without treatment. Others, however, require the regular use of medicated dips or creams until cured. Demodectic mange can be a serious—and incurable—problem in some dogs, especially older dogs. Dogs with demodectic mange should not be used for breeding, since there appears to be a genetic susceptibility to this problem.

At the other extreme, sarcoptic mange is so itchy that dogs can't seem to control themselves from nonstop scratching. This disease, caused by the microscopic scabies or sarcoptic mite, usually causes lesions on the ear, elbows, legs and face. Left untreated, the entire body may be affected, with thick scaly skin and large areas of hair loss. This serious problem spreads rapidly between dogs and may also affect humans. It must be treated immediately!

Then there are chiggers, tiny beasts found primarily in wooded areas, whose activities cause severe itching and reddening of the skin. Chiggers usually prefer the abdomen, neck and head (especially the ear flaps and canals). The correct product to eradicate these mites from your dog must be determined by a veterinarian.

The last mite we'll mention here is the "walking dandruff," or *Chyletiella yasguri*, mite. Usually a problem of puppies, these mites cause a dandrufflike condition most often seen on the head, neck and back. There may be mild itching. When they bite humans, these mites leave itchy red spots similar to flea and scabies lesions. The proper medication readily clears up this problem.

Flies. Irritating fly bites cause scabby, crusty sores on the dog's face and ears. Prick-eared dogs are particularly prone to attack by these pests. The sores frequently bleed episodically until they heal, causing owners as well as dogs a lot of grief. When you know flies are apt to be a problem, protect your dog's skin by applying ordinary insect repellent to vulnerable areas. Be sure to avoid contact with the eyes.

The other problem posed by flies is maggots. First, the flies lay their eggs in the dirty, infected skin and ears of a dog. Next, the maggots hatch and begin ingesting the dog's own flesh. It's a terrible situation which can be prevented from happening in the first place. If your dog is thick coated, keep a close watch on its body to be sure it is not hiding any wounds. Pay special attention to keeping the anal area clean, free of mats and accumulated stool. Wounds on any dog should be cleaned and treated as soon as possible, especially during the summer, to prevent maggot infestation. If this should occur, maggots must be treated promptly by a veterinarian.

Allergies

Unlike humans, the first sign of discomfort usually shown by an allergic dog is itchy, irritated skin. Some dogs also get a runny nose or eyes, sneeze or even suffer from vomiting and diarrhea. Uncovering the source of the allergy can be quite frustrating for owners and veterinarians alike.

Some dogs are allergic to components in their diet. A food allergy can emerge early in life; usually the offenders are beef or soy products. The best way to determine if diet is causing an allergic reaction is to feed hypoallergenic food for several weeks and see if the signs regress. To be altogether certain of a food allergy, you'd need to challenge the dog with the prior food and see if the signs recur.

Another common allergic condition is known as atopy. Atopy refers to an inhalant allergy or a reaction to environmental components. Molds, plants, dust, even furniture stuffing fall into this category. Signs of atopy may be seasonal. The only practical way to discover what's bothering this allergic dog is to ask a veterinary dermatologist to conduct an intradermal skin test, much as is done with human allergy sufferers. Then you can try avoiding offensive material, or attempt hyposensitization. These problems are also best discussed with a qualified dermatologist.

A few comments about some common dog allergies: many dogs are sensitive to flea collars, flea bites or dyes in plastic food dishes. These things are easily identified and corrected. If a flea collar irritates your dog's neck, remove it and wash the area thoroughly with a mild shampoo. Switch to another type of product. We have already discussed remedies for dealing with fleas, and therefore flea bite allergies.

Finally, see if your dog's red, irritated nose is caused by an allergy to dyed plastic by replacing the plastic dish with metal or glass. If it's an allergy, the condition should be resolved.

Hot Spots

One of the most common summertime complaints seen by veterinarians are hot spots, round hairless patches of tender, red, oozing skin which seem to erupt overnight. They are usually found on the rump, although they may appear anywhere on the body. Hot spots are especially prevalent in heavy-coated breeds and in any dog with skin allergies.

Hot spots probably begin as a focus of irritation caused by a flea bite, impacted anal sacs or other small annoyances. However, the more the dog licks and chews at the spot, the worse it feels, so the more the animal licks and chews. A small problem explodes into a large one. These lesions need to be treated promptly before you have a dog in agony.

Treatment of a hot spot begins with clipping away the surrounding hair and cleaning the surface of the wound. The area is then covered with a soothing spray, liquid or ointment. The veterinarian will attempt to find and eliminate the source of the complaint. Your dog may need to wear an Elizabethan collar (a plastic contraption similar to a lampshade) around his neck, to prevent it from attacking the area further, until the skin begins to heal. Antibiotics and anti-inflammatory medications may be prescribed as well.

Seborrhea

Seborrheic skin is flaky and scaly, and may feel either excessively dry or oily. Secondary infections are not uncommon, especially in the case of oily seborrhea, in which case you may notice a rancid smell emanating from the skin. Seborrhea may be complicated by other problems like hypothyroidism. True seborrhea is an incurable but controllable problem: for example, regular bathing in special shampoos can help eliminate the scaling and oiliness of the skin.

Ringworm

Despite its name, ringworm is not a squirming parasite but rather a fungal infection of the skin. Ringworm lesions appear as circular, hairless patches of scaly skin. Stubby bits of broken grayish hair may be found within and along the edges of these areas. Severely affected dogs may have diseased areas incorporating large portions of the body. To diagnose ringworm, a culture may be taken from a sample of crust and hair. Proper diagnosis and treatment is especially important since ringworm can spread to people, particularly children.

Infections

Skin infections usually result from damage to the skin by a cut, puncture or scrape. If it is a primary infection, however, the most common presentations are single or multiple areas of red patches resembling a rash or small bumps similar to pimples. There may or may not be itching. Skin infections of this type are usually caused by staphylococcus bacteria and may need to be treated with antibiotics or medicated baths.

Ignoring a skin injury may turn a small problem into a large one through bacterial infection. Infected wounds are painful, red and swollen. They feel warm to the touch and may have an abnormal, puslike discharge. A foul odor may originate from the infected wound. Seek appropriate treatment, such as local wound care and antibiotics, for this condition.

Abscesses

An abscess is a collection of pus under the skin where an injury has occurred, usually from a bite or puncture wound. The area is often painful, swollen and red. Abscesses may break open and drain spontaneously, or they may need to be lanced and flushed before proper healing can take place. Never try to squeeze open an abscess. It should be treated by your veterinarian.

Balding

Hair loss, when it is not caused by a parasitic condition, trauma or infection, may result from one of several metabolic disorders. Cushing's syndrome and hypothyroidism are two of the most common.

In Cushing's syndrome, the adrenal glands secrete an excessive amount of cortisol, a hormone. These dogs begin to lose hair on the flank and neck, and may eventually lose hair on the back and sides of the body as well. The skin itself may become thin, scaly and dry, and may darken in places. Other signs include enlargement of the belly. Typical Cushingoid dogs will want to drink, eat and urinate more frequently than normal. A complex disorder, Cushing's syndrome is usually treatable.

Hypothyroidism occurs when an inadequate amount of thyroid hormone is released to the body. Dogs with this disease seem to gain weight easily, appear sluggish and seek out warm spots even during the summer months. Hair changes are most noticeable, and include loss of hair from the flanks and back, increased pigmentation of the skin, scaling and seborrhea. Because the ears are also commonly affected, you'll often see and smell a thick, greasy, yellowish material inside the canals. Hypothyroidism, once confirmed through a simple blood test, is easily controlled with thyroid hormone supplementation.

Color Changes

Some color changes are normal. For instance, some dogs gradually develop spots as they age, usually on areas like the belly, while no other changes are noticed in the skin or body. There are some changes, however, that you should bring to the attention of your veterinarian.

If your dog's skin develops a yellowish cast, for instance, you'll want to have the dog checked out as soon as possible. It may indicate jaundice, which is most often associated with a liver or blood disorder. Jaundice usually accompanies other signs of illness, all of which mean your dog should be examined thoroughly.

Abnormal pallor should also be evaluated by a veterinarian promptly. This usually means anemia, and a veterinarian will attempt to discover the origin of your dog's red blood cell shortage.

Bruising is a normal result of a blunt object injury or, sometimes, having blood drawn. Unexplained or excessive bruising, however, should be discussed with a veterinarian.

Skin will normally undergo hyperpigmentation, or darkening, in response to chronic irritation. If your dog suffers from allergies or any other condition that makes him continually torture the same spot, the skin will eventually thicken and darken to protect itself. The same goes for areas which undergo repeated friction, like the breastbone area of thin-coated dogs or the outer parts of the elbows. These regions will often seem wrinkled, hairless, thick and blackened—all responses to frequent abuse. Calluses on elbows, hocks and hip areas may cause problems if they are allowed to persist. The best way to prevent calluses is to provide soft bedding for your dog at all times.

Lumps and Bumps

Finding a single lump or bump on your dog's skin is not necessarily reason to panic. Most skin masses are not malignant, and once removed, they do not recur. Some are inconsequential and may be left alone. A wart is a good example of this type of bump; ordinarily they may be ignored, unless owners find them unsightly or they cause the dog discomfort because of their location.

However, every abnormal mass discovered in your dog's skin should be a matter for concern. Let a veterinarian decide whether or not to pursue a diagnostic workup. Because malignancies are a consideration, especially in older dogs, don't waste time before seeking veterinary advice.

The Respiratory System

The respiratory system includes those organs involved in the process of breathing. These involve parts you can see, like the nose and mouth, as well as internal organs such as the trachea, bronchi and lungs.

Problems with respiration may originate anywhere along this pathway. Symptoms of respiratory distress include nasal discharge, coughing or sneezing. Noisy or difficult breathing also indicates an abnormality, as do any changes in voice quality or irregular sounds that seem to come from the throat or chest.

Kennel Cough

Otherwise known as infectious canine tracheobronchitis, kennel cough is a common respiratory problem in dogs. It readily spreads from one individual to another. Many dogs come down with kennel cough after boarding or some other situation where they have been in close proximity to other dogs. Carriers are often asymptomatic.

Signs include a dry, hacking cough sometimes accompanied by a mild nasal discharge. Most dogs remain bright and alert despite their alarming coughing spells, and will spontaneously recover within a few weeks. However, to be on the safe side, most veterinarians prescribe a short course of antibiotics to protect their patients from further harm. Consider asking for the kennel cough vaccination if your dog is going to be staying in a kennel.

Collapsing Trachea

Usually a disease of small dogs, symptoms of a collapsed trachea include noisy breathing and frequent coughing. Sometimes dogs seem incapable of catching their breath.

The trachea is normally a rigid tube. In an affected dog, however, the trachea is somewhat soft, so it tends to narrow from time to time. This obviously impedes air flow. Most dogs learn to live with their problem, as do their owners, once they understand that it is rarely life threatening. Obesity, stress and pressure on the trachea should be avoided. Surgery can help severely affected animals.

Bronchitis

Bronchitis sometimes develops in dogs already suffering from debilitating respiratory infection. Dogs with bronchitis have a dry, rough cough that may persist for days or even weeks. Coughing fits may be so intense that dogs wind up retching afterward. Although they normally maintain a normal temperature, the general appearance of a dog with bronchitis is poor. Treatment includes antibiotics and rest.

Laryngeal Paralysis

Laryngeal paralysis, a problem of large dogs in their middle to old age, is seen congenitally in Siberian Huskies and Bouviers.

The handsome Standard Schnauzer was developed in Germany and has existed for several centuries. Highly intelligent and devoted to home and family, he adapts easily to any environment. *J. S. Dorl*

A well-trained dog should be the goal of every owner. Training often makes the difference between a satisfying companion and a four-legged nuisance.

Jan Plagenz

The Puli has herded sheep on the plains of Hungary for centuries. He still retains the ability today, and herding trials allow owners to observe and appreciate the breed's original work. *Ivy Ainsworth*

The Cocker Spaniel is America's favorite purebred.

Pets by Paulette

The Pomeranian is another longtime American favorite. This sprightly Toy breed is related to the Keeshond, Samoyed and other dogs of northern type. *Pets by Paulette*

A relative newcomer to America's family of purebreds is the Tibetan Terrier. Considered a symbol of good luck in his homeland, the breed combines a people-pleasing charm with its good looks and convenient size. *Richard Morrison*

Dog show competition is always keen, but good sportsmanship is also a factor. Here the winner of the Sporting Group receives the good wishes of rival handlers. *J. S. Dorl*

Trick training and obedience training are not the same, but it is possible to work with the same dog in both areas. *Soren Wesseltoft*

The Labrador Retriever is treasured both as a family companion and as a gun dog. *Cindy Noland*

The Otterhound is an ancient scent hound whose name describes his purpose. While he may be considered a rarity among dogs, his influence is apparent in the Airedale Terrier, a great favorite of many. *Karen Otto*

A Petit Basset Griffon Vendeen, one of the newest additions to the list of AKC recognized breeds, responds to a "stay" signal from his handler. *D. Davis*

An American Staffordshire Terrier takes the high jump in good style. *Jan Plagenz*

The Border Terrier is a rugged companion, always ready to join in any activity. He comes from the Cheviot Hills which separate England and Scotland. *Jane Donahue*

The Pembroke Welsh Corgi, an ancient breed from South Wales, was used for centuries as a cattle drover. An alert watchdog, he is also an excellent obedience performer.

John Firca

Dog shows attract new adherents every year and many find the shows a perfect family activity. Here a class of Bernese Mountain Dogs furnishes a challenge for the judge. *J. S. Dorl*

In recent years, farmers have turned to ancient livestock-guarding breeds to protect their flocks from human and animal predators. These Kuvaszok are as effective on the western plains as their ancestors were on the Hungarian *puszta*.

The first sign may be occasional noisy breathing, especially when the dog has been excited or exercised. Respiratory difficulty may progress to complete inability to breathe. Sometimes surgery is required to alleviate this problem involving the tissue in the back of the throat.

Foreign Bodies

A foreign body is something inside the dog's body that doesn't belong there. In the respiratory system, a foreign body can be a stick or burr in the nose or anything that is accidentally inhaled. Foreign bodies in the nasal passages cause incessant pawing at the nose and furious sneezing. There may be a nasal discharge, with or without bleeding. Do not attempt to retrieve foreign bodies from this delicate area yourself. A veterinarian will probably need to sedate or anesthetize the dog in order to do a proper job.

If the foreign body has gone beyond the nasal passage, then the dog will have a sudden, intense coughing fit. This unusual event may clear itself without further problems as the dog coughs it up. If not, however, get to the veterinarian as soon as possible.

Elongated Soft Palate

An elongated soft palate is most often seen in short-faced breeds. It causes nasal discharge and noisy breathing because the air passages are obstructed. These dogs typically breathe through the mouth, produce snorting noises and snore while sleeping. Signs are exacerbated by hot weather, physical exertion or other stressful conditions. In most cases, surgery corrects the problem by shortening the soft palate.

Rhinitis

Rhinitis is another word for infection of the nasal passages. Dogs with this problem have a thick, foul-smelling nasal discharge from one or both nostrils. Treatment depends on the origin of the problem; infected maxillary teeth are a common culprit, although it may be more serious than that. Antibiotics are typically used to help clear up the infection.

Pneumonia

A very serious disease that can be caused by a virus, bacteria, allergy or parasite, pneumonia needs to be treated without delay. Signs include coughing, rapid breathing, a high fever and a quick pulse. You may or may not actually hear a rattling or bubbling noise within the dog's chest.

The Musculoskeletal System

The musculoskeletal system supports, protects and moves the dog's body. In addition, the bones provide a site for mineral and fat storage, and house the marrow, which produces red blood cells. When something goes wrong with the muscles, tendons, ligaments or bones, the signs are usually obvious. Limping, weakness, pain or stiffness indicate a problem in the musculo-skeletal system, as do swollen joints or any change in the way your dog moves.

Lameness

There are many reasons why dogs limp. Fractures, dislocations, ligamentous injuries, congenital defects and just plain soreness are merely a few. Most of the time, minor limping disappears if the dog has a couple of days of restricted activity and perhaps aspirin for pain relief. If you suspect that trauma has played a role in causing the lameness, or your dog seems to be in serious discomfort, a quick visit to the veterinarian is in order. X-rays may be necessary to verify the existence of a problem. Sometimes tranquilization is required to obtain a good X-ray image of the area, so try to withhold food from the dog before you go to the veterinarian.

Cranial Cruciate Ligament Injury

This common source of sudden rear leg lameness occurs when one of the ligaments inside the knee joint is injured, usually during exercise. Left untreated, the knee remains painful, and arthritis will probably develop in the joint. It is more likely to occur in overweight, adult dogs. Repairing the ligament is a common surgical technique performed at most veterinary practices.

Hip Dysplasia

We could easily devote pages to hip dysplasia, because it is so common and is so great a source of heartbreak, especially to owners of larger dogs. Hip dysplasia is a congenital defect with potential environmental and nutritional influences. Basically, hip dysplasia is malformation of the hip joint. Dogs with this condition show hip pain, limping or a swaying gait. Some animals develop signs during the rapid growth that occurs from four to nine months of age, while others fall victim later in life. Other indications of hip dysplasia include hearing a clicking noise while the dog walks or noticing the dog wince when its hindquarters are touched. Affected dogs are typically slow to rise from a seated position.

The diagnosis is made through orthopedic examination and X-rays of the hip joints. Affected dogs should be maintained at proper weight, to reduce the carrying load on the hindquarters. Their bedding should be kept in a warm, dry place, and their exercise should be restricted. The development of arthritis is a serious concern for dogs with hip dysplasia. Medication can help alleviate the pain of this disease, but surgery (or euthanasia) is sometimes the only humane choice. Lastly, hip dysplasia is an inherited disease, so dogs with confirmed hip dysplasia should *never* be used for breeding.

Medial Luxating Patella

The patella, or kneecap, is a small saucer of bone that glides up and down in front of the knee joint. Because of functional abnormalities, the patella of some small dogs slides toward the inner leg. Off track, the errant patella causes sudden (and often painless) episodes of limping.

Dogs with this condition may need surgical correction of one or both knees to relieve the problem once and for all. Otherwise, the knee may become arthritic. Obesity as well as excessive exercise should always be avoided, since both will aggravate the problem.

Disc Disease

Bad backs trouble some dogs as they do some people, causing pain and incapacitation. Certain breeds, such as the Dachshund, for example, are more prone to developing disc disease than others. Observable signs of this disease start when the disc, which normally acts as a cushion between the vertebrae composing the backbone, protrudes into the spinal cord area. This very painful condition causes the dog to acutely reduce its activity, hold its head and neck in a stiff position and cry out whenever touched. The dog's legs may seem weak or incoordinated.

Dogs with disc disease must be examined by a veterinarian without delay, to decide whether surgery or medical therapy is warranted. Occasionally, disc disease may cause complete paralysis of the hind end.

Arthritis

The most common form of arthritis in the dog is osteoarthritis, a degenerative disease which causes pain, lameness and stiffness in the joints. It is frequently seen in older dogs, usually in the large breeds. Grating between joint surfaces may be felt when the limbs are manipulated. X-rays clearly show changes in the bone itself. Aspirin and other medication may provide some relief. A dog suffering from arthritis must have access to soft bedding in a warm, dry environment. Restricted physical activity is essential and the dog must not become overweight.

The Heart

The rhythmic pumping of the muscular heart circulates blood through the body. Blood provides the body with vital nutrients like oxygen, electrolytes and hormones, which regulate body functions. It also carries away the waste products of metabolism, including carbon dioxide. Heart disease may be either acquired (developed after birth) or congenital (present at birth). Specialized equipment like the EKG and echocardiograph, as well as X-rays and auscultation, may be necessary to determine the exact nature of each form of heart disease.

Each time you visit the veterinarian, he or she should check your dog's heart for abnormal sounds and for irregularities in rhythm or frequency of beats. The pulse should also be evaluated for strength and synchronicity with each contraction of the heart.

Signs which may indicate a heart problem are coughing and shortness of breath, lethargy, weakness and distended abdomen and/or swollen limbs. If your dog suffers from fainting spells, stunted growth, weight loss or if you notice a bluish color of its gums, be sure to seek veterinary advice.

Congestive Heart Failure

Heart failure occurs when the heart can't deliver a sufficient quantity of oxygenated blood to meet the body's demands. The term "congestive" refers to an abnormal amount of fluid accumulating outside of the vessels, as in the lungs. When this happens, for example, the dog may begin to cough and show shortness of breath. It may be unable to tolerate excitement or exercise, and the abdomen may start to enlarge as fluid accumulates in this body compartment as well. Congestive heart failure, once diagnosed, may be treated with drugs to strengthen contractions of the heart, expand the vascular capacity and promote excretion of retained fluids through diuresis. Feeding a special low-salt diet is usually recommended to help lessen problems of fluid retention.

Heartworm Disease

This disease is caused by actual worms inhabiting the chambers of the heart. Heartworms, you may recall from our earlier discussion, gain entry to the dog's circulatory system through the bite of a carrier mosquito. Eventually, adult worms migrate to the heart and arteries leading to the lungs. Since worms may grow to twelve inches long, it is not surprising that they both physically obstruct blood flow and damage the pulmonary arteries, making it difficult for the heart to pump blood through the lungs. Heart failure and severe lung damage can occur in heavily infested dogs. Heartworm disease can be treated with arsenic-containing drugs to eradicate the adult worms, followed by other drugs to kill immature worms, and long periods of forced rest. It's better to prevent heartworm infestation in the first place by giving preventative medications during the warm months of the year.

Cardiomyopathy

Canine dilated (congested) cardiomyopathy is a disease of large and giant breeds, usually observed in one to six year olds. The heart muscle weakens and degenerates, making blood flow sluggish and resulting in generalized congestive heart failure. The heart itself is greatly enlarged, and is predisposed to irregularities in heart rate. Some heartbeats may actually fail to eject blood into the system. Signs of cardiomyopathy include fatigue, coughing, distention of the abdomen, weight loss and occasionally swollen legs. Collapse may occur. Drugs can help prolong life, but this is only temporary, since the dramatic changes in the heart are themselves incurable.

Chronic Valvular Disease

Valves are tiny pieces of tissue that, by rhythmically snapping open and shut, regulate the flow of blood through the heart. A common form of heart disease, chronic valvular disease occurs when the valves thicken and fail to seal tightly, allowing blood to leak backward. Gradually, the defect compromises the heart's ability to pump, and heart failure develops. Signs of this insufficiency are coughing, difficult or noisy breathing and restlessness at night. The veterinarian will usually detect a heart murmur.

Congenital Heart Diseases

Congenital heart diseases are functional cardiac problems that are present at birth. Your first indication of a defect may occur at the time of the puppy's initial veterinary examination, when abnormal heart sounds are detected. Heart failure may also present itself at an early stage. Here are just a few examples of potential defects.

One form of congenital heart defect is patent ductus arteriosus. This refers to the presence of a vessel—which should ordinarily close shortly after birth—connecting the pulmonary artery to the aorta. The vessel gives blood a way to bypass the lungs, so there's less oxygenated blood going to the body. A distinct heart murmur is noticed upon ausculting the chest. The only effective treatment is surgical repair.

Ventricular septal defects also occur in newborn pups. These are small openings in the muscular wall separating the two major pumping chambers of the heart. The hole can vary in size. Surgical correction is possible at specialized veterinary institutions.

A constrictive abnormality which obstructs the passage of blood out of the right ventricle into the pulmonary artery is known as pulmonic stenosis. This defect increases the workload of the heart and may cause heart failure. Some types of stenosis can be partially relieved by surgery.

The Gastrointestinal System

The gastrointestinal system takes in and processes food, providing energy for sustaining life. The major organs include the stomach and intestines.

Disturbances of the gastrointestinal system probably account for more visits, outside of vaccinations, to veterinarians than anything else. It's virtually certain that someday, during the course of your dog's lifetime, it will suffer a bout of vomiting and/or diarrhea. Other signs of gastrointestinal upset include regurgitation, constipation, unusual stools or flatulence. Because a dog with a gastrointestinal disturbance usually feels uncomfortable, it may act restless or drool excessively, or need to drink or urinate more frequently than normal.

Vomiting

Dogs vomit for a myriad of reasons. Some are more serious than others. If your dog vomits once or twice but seems healthy in every other respect, there is probably no need to worry. Occasional uncomplicated vomiting is caused by change of diet, garbage ingestion or eating plant material. If you restrict food for a day and give your dog a little Pepto-Bismol, the problem will probably disappear on its own. Feed a bland diet such as baby food or boiled hamburger combined with plain white rice (pour the fat off before you mix the two together) for a few days more.

If, however, a dog has frequent or forceful vomiting, or vomits in conjunction with other signs such as diarrhea, depression or collapse, get the animal to the veterinarian. This also goes for vomiting in which blood or other unusual substances are observed. Potential causes for these types of vomiting may include viral infections, foreign body obstructions, tumors, pancreatitis, renal or liver disease and so forth.

Diarrhea

Diarrhea is another common symptom in dogs. Mild diarrhea is often treatable at home when it occurs in dogs showing no other signs of illness. Persistent diarrhea, however, means a visit to your veterinarian is warranted. Bring a sample of the stool with you for analysis. If this is impossible, be sure you can give the veterinarian an accurate description of the stool's appearance, amount and frequency of production. This information can give clues to the origin of the problem.

Many of the reasons dogs come down with uncomplicated diarrhea are comparable to our discussion of vomiting. Unfamiliar food or consuming something indigestible are frequent causes, not to mention stress. More serious reasons include viral gastroenteritis such as coronavirus or parvovirus, for which there are vaccinations. A dog with diarrhea should always be checked for the presence of internal parasites such as worms, coccidia and giardia.

To treat mild diarrhea at home, withhold food for twenty-four hours. You may offer small quantities of water. Give the dog Kaopectate or Pepto-Bismol to soothe the intestinal tract. You can start feeding a bland diet the next day. The one described for treating vomiting dogs is fine. If the diarrhea does not respond to this therapy, your veterinarian should be consulted.

Constipation

A dog is constipated if it hasn't passed any stool for a day or two. In addition, the dog may strain to defecate without producing any stool. Constipated dogs are often listless, inappetent or may begin to vomit if the condition is allowed to persist. Occasionally, a constipated dog may pass watery or bloody material reminiscent of diarrhea despite the fact that the colon is packed with hard stool.

Constipation can occur secondary to eating a diet low in fiber or from ingesting bone chips, grass, paper or other indigestible material. Sometimes constipation can result from an enlarged prostate gland, a hernia or an inherent problem with the colon. Some dogs seem to be constipation-prone, and must be monitored closely to be sure they pass stool regularly. Other dogs, particularly those with long hair, become mechanically constipated because mats around their anus completely block the passage of feces. Make sure this doesn't happen to your long-haired dog.

An enema may be needed to soften the stool and allow its expulsion. You may elect to have this done at the veterinary clinic. If you choose to do it at home, a soapy warm water enema is the safest to administer.

A change of diet to include the addition of bran or other fiber-containing substances may help chronically constipated dogs. Commercial dog foods are available to serve this purpose. The veterinarian may also instruct you to add water to your dog's dry food. In addition, you may be advised to withhold bones from your dog.

Bloat

Bloat (acute gastric dilation-torsion) can happen so fast and often proves so deadly the dog is gone before you know it. A disease of large, deep-chested dogs, bloat occurs when the stomach fills with gas and/or fluids, then swells and sometimes twists on its own axis. Dogs often go into shock when this happens. Bloat needs to be treated immediately if the dog's life is to be saved.

The history of a dog with bloat often indicates that the dog ate a large meal, drank lots of water and then exercised within two to three hours after eating. The first sign shown by a dog with impending bloat is often restlessness. The belly appears swollen and firm; tapping gently on it may produce a drumlike sound.

Immediate surgery is a dog's best chance for survival. The procedure will quickly decompress the stomach and correct any torsion by repositioning the stomach within the abdomen. Intravenous fluids need to be administered to bolster circulation.

Diet and management changes alone will not protect every dog from bloat. You can try to help your dog, however, by following these suggestions: 1. Feed small meals, two or three times daily, instead of one large meal, or make dry food available throughout the day and allow the dog to eat at will. 2. Restrict water intake after feeding. 3. Never exercise the dog immediately after it has eaten. If dry food is offered two or three times daily, add water to it first and let the food get soggy so the dog's stomach fills faster and it won't want to drink as much.

Pancreatic Exocrine Insufficiency

The typical dog with pancreatic exocrine insufficiency (PEI) has an enormous appetite but never seems to gain weight. Its stools are usually voluminous, soft, light colored, and may appear greasy or oily due to high amounts of undigested fats and proteins. Dogs with PEI are unable to produce certain enzymes in the pancreas, enzymes which would promote normal digestion and absorption of nutrients. PEI is treated with lifelong supplementation of pancreatic enzymes, usually added directly to the food, along with the feeding of a low fat, moderate protein diet.

Flatulence

Flatulence can occur after feeding dogs onions, beans, cauliflower, cabbage, soybeans or other highly fermentable foods. The same applies for diets that include a lot of milk or meat. You may discover that changing the dog's diet will improve the situation. If not, offering a small amount of Digel (simethicone containing antacid) may provide temporary relief. If all else fails, have your dog checked out for any contributing health problems.

Eating Stool

Coprophagy, or eating stools, is not uncommon, especially in young dogs. Nevertheless, this objectionable and unhealthy habit should be discouraged. Adding meat tenderizer to the dog's food works wonders for some dogs, presumably because it imparts a bad flavor to the fecal material. Sometimes changing the diet can solve the problem. If nothing helps, have a veterinarian examine the dog for some form of dietary deficiency. In the meantime, always make your displeasure clear to the dog who eats stools. When you catch the dog in the act, administer an immediate and firm correction.

Anal Irritation

The dog who bites and licks incessantly at the anus or scoots its behind along the floor may be suffering from one of several problems. If soft stools were recently experienced, the anus may be irritated and inflamed secondary to fecal soiling. Some dogs are bothered by insect bites (fleas, for example) or intestinal parasites. A common source of irritation is impaction of the anal sacs.

Finding and eliminating the cause are the first steps to remedying the problem. Meanwhile, provide relief by gently cleaning the anal area using warm, soapy water and applying petroleum jelly or similar soothing salve as needed.

The Eyes, Ears and Mouth

The eyes, ears and mouth are the organs of sight, sound, and taste. The mouth also aids in respiration and initiates the chain of events that brings nourishment to the rest of the body.

The eyes, ears and mouth are common sites for problems in the dog. General types of signs to watch for include abnormal discharges, inflammation, swelling, growths or sensitivity to stimulus. Consult a veterinarian if your dog experiences apparent vision loss, excessive tearing from the eyes or abnormal color within or around the eye. An ear problem is indicated by foul odors emanating from the canal, scratching at the ears, hearing loss, head shaking or head tilt. A problem with the mouth is suspected when dogs exhibit unusual drooling or oral discharge, head shaking, bleeding or pawing at the mouth. Bad breath, inflammation, growths or difficulty in swallowing may also point toward oral disease.

THE EYE

Watery Eyes

Excessive tearing is seen most often in the small breeds. The resulting moisture around the eyes and down the sides of the face contribute to local inflammation or infection of the underlying skin. The discharge often stains surrounding hair an ugly brown color; this is especially obvious in white or light-colored dogs.

Watery eyes are due to a variety of causes, the most common being irritation to the eye and inadequate tear drainage. Removing the source of the irritation, such as excessive hair around the eyes, treating infection with antibiotics or flushing the nasolacrimal drainage system can help eliminate the problem.

Entropion and Ectropion

Entropion and ectropion are eyelid abnormalities. In the former, the eyelid (usually the lower lid) rolls toward the eye, permitting the lashes to rub against the cornea and irritate this sensitive structure. Entropion may result from an eyelid injury, but it also occurs as a congenital defect.

The inverse of entropion, ectropion is an eyelid that rolls away from the eyeball. It is usually a problem of dogs with loose facial skin. Ectropion also results from injury or birth defect, or loss of muscle tone in the older dog. Insufficiently protected by this loose eyelid, the eyes of a dog with ectropion are extremely vulnerable to irritation. Corrective surgery is available to repair either of these two eyelid problems.

Cherry Eye

All dogs have a tear gland on the inner surface of their third eyelid (the pink membrane that rises from the corner of the eye while your dog is asleep). Occasionally, the gland flips up and protrudes from the corner of the eye. The red, smooth, cherry-like lump doesn't seem to bother most dogs in the least, but can be extremely alarming for owners. Most cases of cherry eye need surgery to either replace or remove the gland.

Conjunctivitis

Conjunctivitis is the inflammation of the fleshy membrane which lines the eyelids and covers part of the eyeball. Signs include reddening or swelling of the tissue around the eye and a watery or thick ocular discharge. Conjunctivitis can be bacterial, viral or allergic in origin, or can result from irritation (a foreign body, for instance, or even a strong gust of wind to the eye). Usually, the problem is readily solved once the cause is identified and appropriate treatment is started.

Corneal Ulcer

The cornea is the clear membrane over the pupil of the eye where, in humans, a contact lens is placed. When something causes a nick or break in that membrane, an ulcer is likely to occur. Ulcers are very painful. Dogs usually hold the affected eye tightly shut, and you will notice an ocular discharge. When examined, the cornea typically looks cloudy in the area of the injury. Corneal ulcers need to be treated without delay to prevent serious complications such as loss of vision.

Glaucoma

Glaucoma is caused by increased pressure within the eyeball. As the pressure climbs, tissues within the eyes are destroyed, leading to partial or complete blindness. Dogs with glaucoma may squint or stare; the eyes seem to be enlarged, with reddening of the white part of the eye (the sclera) and a hazy appearance to the inside of the eye. This serious condition is quite painful, and requires immediate veterinary attention.

Dry Eye

Some dogs lack adequate tear production to lubricate and protect the eyes, resulting in keratitis sicca or dry eye. Damage to the cornea may occur. Dry eye is easily diagnosed by measuring tear production on a tiny strip of absorbent paper. It is usually treated with artificial tears, a solution placed in the eye several times daily. Alternatively, a surgical procedure to redirect one of the salivary ducts can help some dogs to lubricate the eyes.

Cataracts

Cataracts affect the lens, an internal part of the eye which focuses vision. Relatively common in older dogs, cataracts are readily apparent as distinct opacities (like small marbles) set deep within the eye. Because predisposition to cataract may be an inherited defect, cataracts can actually occur at any age in dogs, and they may also occur secondary to diabetes. The degree of vision loss varies from individual to individual. When blindness is significant, surgical removal of the lens may restore functional vision.

Progressive Retinal Atrophy

Progressive retinal atrophy (PRA) is a genetic disease in which the cells of the retina gradually degenerate, leading to loss of sight. Many breeds are affected by this devastating disease. Predicting the onset of blindness is breed dependent, but it may occur at from several months to several years of age.

The first indication of PRA is loss of night vision. With dogs, owners first notice behavioral changes linked to situations in which light is limited. The disease then progresses over a period of months to years, but the outcome is blindness. Unfortunately, there is no known treatment for PRA.

THE EAR

Ear Infections

External ear infections are common, especially in dogs with pendulous ears or ears that contain a lot of hair. The dark, moist environment inherent in these ears encourages bacterial or fungal overgrowth. Parasites, excessive wax, allergies or foreign material within the ear can also lead to ear problems. Some breeds and individuals are more prone to recurrences of these problems than others.

An infected ear is painful, swollen and malodorous. The dog may paw at the ear, shake its head or hold its head tilted toward the ground on the affected side. If you look inside the ear, you may see either dark or puslike material oozing out of the ear canal. The ear will need to be cleaned and medicated, possibly under anesthesia, to remove the discharge as well as any foreign material within the canal. Chronic ear infections are not uncommon. Some cases are best treated surgically to permanently improve exposure to the ear canal for cleaning, circulation of air and drainage.

Ear Mites

Ear mites are microscopic parasites of the ear canals, where a characteristic coffee ground–like discharge heralds their presence. An intensely itchy condition, ear mite infections are treated with a parasiticidal ear ointment, frequently administered daily for several weeks. Flea powder may also be necessary to kill any mites which have traveled beyond the ear canals.

Aural Hematoma

Aural hematomas are soft swellings that suddenly appear when bleeding has occurred within the cartilage of the ear flap. Rarely painful in themselves, they are usually associated with another problem of the ear such as an infection or injury that caused the dog to violently shake or scratch its head. An autoimmune problem may be at fault. Simple drainage will not solve the problem. Most hematomas are surgically opened to remove the blood clot, and then stitched flat until they heal. In fact, left untreated, the blood clot will resolve on its own, but a contracted cauliflower ear will remain.

Deafness

Dogs lose their ability to hear from injury, infection, drug reactions, excessive noise or simply old age. They may also be born deaf or suffer from gradual hearing loss because of a congenital defect. One or both ears may be affected.

Unless complete, deafness is hard to assess in dogs. Obvious signs include difficulty in rousing a dog, or failure of the dog to respond to loud noises made outside its field of vision. With prompt detection, deafness is occasionally curable, as in bacterial infections of the middle or inner ear, or surgical removal of an obstruction in the ear canal. Also, deafness associated with trauma or loud noise may resolve with time.

THE MOUTH

Gingivitis and Dental Disease

Poor oral hygiene causes gum and tooth disease in many dogs. In addition, some breeds seem inherently prone to these problems. Dogs in need of help have blatant signs: the teeth look terrible, the gums are swollen and may bleed easily, the breath smells foul and you may see excessive drooling. When the roots of the rear teeth are affected, facial swelling commonly occurs.

Regular oral inspection and dental cleaning is important. See pages 62–64 for a discussion on brushing the teeth at home. Despite your best efforts, however, professional cleaning will probably be needed from time to time. Also, some oral diseases are linked to more serious problems like diabetes or kidney disease.

Lip Fold Infection

This problem affects dogs with loose skin around the mouth, where small pools of food and saliva accumulate. It also happens when mouth injuries become infected, or when licking spreads an infection from another part of the body to the mouth. If your dog begins to drool a thick, odorous substance or paws at its mouth, check the skin around the lips. Always try to keep the lip folds as clean as possible, especially following a meal, to prevent the onset of an infection.

Burns

Oral burns are not unusual, since dogs use their mouths to investigate many new and seemingly tasty objects. Mild oral burns will usually heal themselves. More serious burns, particularly those which occur from ingesting chemical substances, must be brought to the attention of a veterinarian.

Foreign Bodies

Foreign bodies, such as sticks, frequently become lodged in the mouth, especially across the palate, causing dogs to suddenly paw frantically at their mouths and drool or gag. They may shake their heads and refuse to eat until the object is detected and removed. If you can't locate the trouble, bring the dog to a professional.

The Neurological System

The neurological system is composed of the brain, spinal cord and nerves. It receives, conducts and interprets sensory information and distributes messages that control the activity of muscles and other organs. Incoordination, weakness, changes in muscle tone and paralysis are signs of a neurological problem. Other indications include seizures, sensory abnormalities and sudden bizarre behavior changes.

Seizures

Seizures are frequently caused by epilepsy, although they may be due to viral, bacterial or fungal infections as well as brain tumors or head trauma. During seizures, dogs typically appear to lose consciousness, fall on their sides, vocalize, paddle their legs and frequently urinate and/or defecate (although any bizarre behavior can be part of a seizure).

Epilepsy occurs when a focus in the brain suddenly fires for no apparent reason, setting off a flurry of messages in the sensitive brain tissue. Although seizures are distressing to observe, especially for the first time, most are rarely life threatening. A dog exhibiting seizures should be examined thoroughly by a veterinarian to try to determine their cause. If the diagnosis is epilepsy, oral medication (usually phenobarbital) can help minimize the recurrence of seizures.

Rabies

Rabies is caused by a virus transmitted by contact with infected saliva, usually from the bite of a rabid animal (skunks, foxes, bats and raccoons are typical carriers). There is little chance of survival once the virus starts reproducing within the body. Dogs are a primary source of rabies in man; you must maintain up-to-date rabies vaccinations in your dog.

The first sign of rabies in an infected animal is usually a marked personality change. In contrast to its ordinary behavior, the dog may seem overly affectionate or shy; it may appear restless or become aggressive. Many dogs become sensitive to light, their eyes dilated. In addition, they often run a fever, have diarrhea or vomit.

Dogs with the paralytic form of rabies lose their muscle control, so the jaw may hang down and the tongue may protrude. The dog may drool, cough, paw at the mouth or demonstrate a voice change. Eventually the rabid dog loses coordination, collapses, enters a coma and dies. There is no treatment for rabies in the dog.

Distemper

Dogs are routinely vaccinated for immunity against distemper. However, distemper still affects dogs whose owners have not sought to protect their dogs from this virus. Neurological signs of distemper include epilepticlike seizures, snapping of the jaws and uncontrollable twitching. A thick, yellow discharge from the nose and eyes is observed, and there is a dry cough. Vomiting and diarrhea may also occur. Recovery is possible, but unlikely, once neurological signs are evident.

Paralysis

Partial or complete paralysis may be caused by several diseases in dogs. One of the most common, outside of traumatic injury, is intervertebral disc disease. The problem arises when discs apply pressure on the spinal cord (see Musculoskeletal Diseases). Neurological messages between the brain and body parts are affected, and paralysis may follow.

Other degenerative diseases that involve changes in the spine, most often observed in large breeds, can cause paralysis, as can growing tumors and disorders of the peripheral nerves. A veterinarian will need to perform a special neurological examination, in conjunction with other diagnostic tests, to determine the origin of the paralysis.

The Urinary System

The urinary system includes the kidneys and ureters, bladder, prostate (in male dogs) and urethra. The kidneys are the major organs, maintaining correct water and mineral balance and excreting waste products of metabolism.

Excessive drinking and urination are often the first signs observed by owners of dogs with urological problems. Other signs include straining or inability to urinate, frequent urination of small amounts, blood in the urine and uncontrollable urination. Dogs with kidney pain will sometimes stand in a hunched-up posture. Weight loss, inappetence and vomiting are also potential indications of kidney disease.

Chronic Kidney Failure

Kidney failure can happen at any stage of a dog's life, but it is much more common in older dogs. Typical signs include excessive drinking and urination, weight and appetite loss and vomiting. As waste products accumulate in the blood, the dog becomes listless, weak and depressed. Without therapy, dogs with kidney failure will die. One of the primary therapeutic measures for kidney failure is intravenous fluid therapy, which requires hospitalization. Kidney disease, whether congenital or acquired, usually carries a grave prognosis for a normal life expectancy.

Bladder Infection

Bladder infections, or cystitis, frequently occur in both male and female dogs. Individuals suffering from cystitis typically urinate more frequently than normal, usually in small amounts, and blood may be clearly visible in the urine. Urination may appear difficult or painful. Females may also have a vaginal discharge and lick their genital area frequently. A urine sample, sometimes a sterile specimen, is needed to diagnose the problem. Because cystitis is usually caused by a bacterial infection, antibiotics are commonly prescribed for its treatment.

Bladder Stones

Symptoms that suggest the presence of bladder stones are straining or inability to pass urine, recurrent bladder infections or dribbling urine. Male dogs are most apt to suffer from urinary blockage because their urinary tract is narrow. Some breeds, such as the Dalmatian, have increased incidence of producing bladder stones. Most stones can be readily identified with an X-ray of the abdomen.

Urinary obstruction is very serious and needs to be relieved as soon as possible via catheterization. Surgery may be required to remove the stones, and medications or dietary restrictions may be prescribed to help prevent further stones from forming.

Prostatitis

Non-neutered male dogs may encounter prostatic enlargement or infection (prostatitis), showing signs of difficult or painful urination. Dogs with prostatitis are ordinarily feverish, drip blood or pus from the preputial opening, and may stand in a pained, hunched-up posture. A bacterial infection, prostatitis is treated with appropriate antibiotics. It can become chronic in some male dogs.

The Reproductive System

The reproductive system includes the sexual organs, both internal and external, of male and female dogs. Infertility is only one indication of a problem with this system. Other symptoms include abnormal discharge from the penis or vulva, and swelling, inflammation or pain involving the reproductive organs.

Undescended Testicles

Both testicles should be in the scrotum by the time a puppy is six months old. Failure of one or both testicles to descend is abnormal, and the affected individual has a higher risk of developing testicular tumors later in life. These dogs should be neutered (the surgeon will locate and remove the "missing" testicle)—both for the dog's health and for the prevention of breeding, since this defect can be inherited.

Mammary Gland Tumors

Tumors of the mammary gland, or breast, are among the most common neoplasms found in female dogs. Approximately half of the tumors are malignant. Remember that this type of cancer is almost entirely preventable by spaying a bitch when she is young.

Mammary gland tumors usually appear as small, firm nodules located most often in the nipples nearest to the hind legs. They can occur singly or in groups, and may exhibit rapid growth. Owners of unspayed bitches should examine their dog's abdomen regularly and bring any lumps to the attention of a veterinarian. Surgery is usually performed to remove the tumors. A biopsy will determine whether the tissue is malignant or benign. Veterinarians usually X-ray the dog's chest prior to surgery to check for evidence of related cancer in the lungs.

Pyometra

Another disease of the unspayed bitch, pyometra is a serious uterine infection in which the uterus fills up with pus. It is usually seen in females over six years old, but can occasionally occur in younger animals. Pus may be clearly visible emerging from the bitch's genitals.

Bitches affected with pyometra are commonly depressed, and may vomit. Related signs are increased thirst and frequency of urination. Pyometra can be fatal if it is not treated promptly. Usually, emergency surgery to remove the infected uterus is required. Other methods of treatment are occasionally tried for valuable bitches intended for breeding. Again, spaying eliminates the possibility of pyometra—once and for all!

Vaginal Infection

Female dogs who lick excessively at their genitals and produce an abnormal vaginal discharge which stains the hair around the vulva may have vaginitis. These bitches may also seem unusually attractive to male dogs. In young females, the infection may be characterized by only small amounts of discharge and signs of painful urination. Antibiotics and douches are used to treat the problem.

Infection of the Penis

Most mature male dogs normally discharge a small amount of white or yellowish material from the skin covering the penis, known as the prepuce. However, if a dog licks frequently at the prepuce, or produces an excessive, discolored or odorous discharge, then an infection of the penis (balanoposthitis) is likely. The penis may appear intensely red and be covered with small bumps. Antibiotics and douches are commonly used to eliminate the infection.

Inflammation of the Testicle

Orchitis, or inflammation of the testicle, may result from an external injury or internal disease. The outcome of this painful condition may be infertility. Inflamed testicles appear firm and enlarged. They are extremely sensitive. The dog shows difficulty in walking and may prefer to sit on cold surfaces. Orchitis must be treated promptly to preserve fertility in a breeding dog.

Testicular Tumors

There are three general types of testicular tumors, with varying potential for malignancy. If you notice any change in the appearance or consistency of your dog's testicles, have the dog examined by a veterinarian. The treatment for testicular tumors is castration.

Brucellosis

Canine brucellosis is a bacterial disease spread from one dog to another through close physical contact or ingestion of infected material. Reproductive failure, chiefly abortion, is the main sign of infection. Affected dogs may appear depressed, with a poor coat, enlarged lymph nodes and swollen joints. Alternatively, there may be no signs of illness at all. Infected male dogs may suffer from inflammation of the scrotum, testicles or prostate. Dogs who abort or who have difficulty in conceiving should be tested for brucellosis. No effective vaccine has yet been discovered to prevent this disease.

· 9 ·

FIRST AID

$\mathbf{F}$IRST AID IS the immediate action taken in an emergency before you can reach a veterinarian. It can help prevent injuries from worsening, alleviate pain or even save your dog's life. First aid, however, is a *preliminary* measure—it should never replace professional care.

The following pages describe what to do in some common emergencies. However, if you find you must use these recommendations, you are likely to also need veterinary help at the earliest possible moment. First aid situations usually call for fast action. Don't panic.

Be prepared. Familiarize yourself with first aid techniques before an actual crisis happens. The telephone number of your veterinarian or veterinary emergency hospital should always be posted near the phone, along with your other emergency numbers. Notify the emergency veterinarian that you are on your way with an animal and describe the nature of the problem so preparations can be made for your arrival. Actions such as these can greatly improve your pet's chances for survival.

Restraint

Even a loving and trusted dog may bite when hurt and frightened. The best way to ensure your safety while trying to help or restrain an injured dog is to apply a muzzle.

Constructing an emergency muzzle with panty hose, a gauze bandage, a necktie or piece of rope about two feet long is not difficult. Begin by tying a loose knot in the middle of the material, leaving a large loop. Then slip the loop over the dog's snout and tighten the knot over the bridge of the nose. Bring the ends down under the chin, tie a knot there, and then bring the ends around back of the ears. Finish by securely tying a bow behind the ears. The muzzle will not interfere with breathing if tied in this manner, and can be released quickly by loosening the bow and pulling the material straight from the nose.

Transporting an Injured Dog

An injured dog must be carried so that further damage is avoided. Dogs of any size may be placed on a towel or blanket, which is then lifted by its edges. Or they may be gently laid on a firm surface of sufficient size, such as a plywood board, before being transported. Smaller dogs can be wrapped gently in warm material and carried in one's arms or carried in a sturdy box.

Always exercise caution when attempting to pick up and support an injured animal. If you haven't muzzled the dog, it may try to bite you, or you may inadvertently worsen matters by carrying it improperly. As always, use common sense.

Artificial Respiration

Artificial respiration is necessary when a dog has stopped breathing. Be extremely careful, since your face will be very close to the dog's mouth (and teeth). Even dogs in respiratory arrest can reflexively close their jaws without warning.

Open the dog's mouth and check for obstructions. Extend the dog's tongue and look into the throat and make sure that, too, is clear. Remove any fluid from the mouth that might interfere with the passage of air. Then close the mouth and continue to hold it gently closed.

Now inhale. Completely cover the dog's nose with your mouth and exhale gently; don't blow hard! Carefully force air into the lungs and watch the chest for expansion. Repeat every five to six seconds, or ten to twelve breaths per minute.

Heart Massage

Heart massage is attempted when you can't detect a heartbeat. It should be combined with artificial respiration. A basic course in CPR will help you learn how to perform this potentially lifesaving technique on both animals and people.

To begin, lay the dog on its right side, and place two hands over the heart area. Press firmly on the chest about seventy times per minute. In the case of a small dog, place one hand on either side of the chest near the elbow instead. Try to keep your wits, and avoid breaking the dog's ribs by pressing too hard as you try to reestablish a heartbeat.

Bleeding

External bleeding may be controlled by applying a pressure dressing, which you can make out of strips of gauze or other sturdy fabric. Wrap the injured area in your bandage material, applying even pressure as you work. Watch for tissue swelling below the wound, a sign of blocked circulation. Should this happen, you must loosen or remove the bandage. Avoid using elasticized bandage material, if possible.

If no bandage material is available, place pressure directly on the wound with your hand or a clean piece of cloth to help block the flow of blood.

When serious bleeding occurs, such as when an artery has been severed, you may need to apply a tourniquet in addition to a pressure bandage. Tourniquets may be fashioned from loops of rope, gauze or cloth—anything that can be wrapped tightly around the area above the wound to interrupt the blood supply. If you are forced to use a tourniquet, you must loosen the pressure every ten minutes or so, or else the tissues will suffer from lack of oxygen.

Shock

Shock is characterized by collapse of the cardiovascular system. Signs of shock include a rapid, weak heartbeat, dilated pupils, pale gums and overall weakness; shock demands immediate emergency attention.

Dogs suffer from shock most often as a result of being hit by a car or any other massive injury. It can also occur secondary to serious disease.

Time is precious in treating an animal in shock. Take whatever measures are immediately required, such as controlling hemorrhage, while you transport the dog to an emergency facility. Try to keep the dog as quiet and warm (animals in shock commonly have low body temperature) as possible.

Fractures

Fractured bones are very painful but not always immediately obvious. If you suspect your dog has a fracture, carefully transport it to the veterinarian on a rigid board or use other means of support, avoiding stress on the injured area. If a limb is fractured, position it on a cushion, wrap it in a rolled up magazine or just gently support it in your hand (muzzle the dog as a precaution!) to avoid more serious injury.

Compound fractures, characterized by the bone piercing the skin, are more serious and more susceptible to infection. Immediately cover the area with as clean a piece of material as you can find and then get emergency help.

Heatstroke

Heatstroke affects dogs whose body temperatures climb way above normal range. Tragically, most cases of heatstroke occur when owners close their dogs in cars with the windows rolled up, or confine them to other poorly ventilated areas, on hot, humid days. It only takes a few minutes for heatstroke to develop.

A dog with heatstroke breathes rapidly but takes shallow breaths. The heartbeat is also very rapid. If not already collapsed, the dog looks close to it. The body temperature is typically well above 104 degrees. It is crucial to cool an animal suffering from heatstroke as quickly as possible and treat shock and other complications which accompany this condition.

The most effective way to begin lowering the dog's temperature is to spray it with cool water and place ice against the groin,
belly, head and neck. Wrap cold, wet towels around the entire
body; seek immediate veterinary help.

And by all means, always make sure an animal has adequate
ventilation, shade and water during hot weather. If you must
leave the dog in a car, even for just a few minutes, leave the
windows open wide enough to provide circulating air (but not
wide enough to allow the dog to escape). Or leave the motor and
air conditioner running. Better yet, leave the dog at home.

Poisons

When seeking assistance for the treatment of poisoning, a few
simple facts are extremely helpful: *what* the dog ate, *how much*
got into its system, and *how long ago* the ingestion occurred. This
information will greatly facilitate the veterinarian's plan of action.

You should also keep the number of a local poison control
center near the phone at all times. Furthermore, bring any information you have about the substance—the container, label,
drug insert, whatever—along with you to the veterinarian.

Let's look at some of the most common types of poisoning in
dogs.

Insecticides (such as flea and tick preparations). The most
common signs shown by dogs who are poisoned by these products are trembling, weakness, drooling, vomiting and loss of
bowel control. The situation may be very serious. Immediately
remove any flea collar or chemical-containing material from the
dog's body or environment, rinse off any dip that might have
been applied and call the veterinarian for advice. Never use
more than the recommended amount, strength or number of
products at any one time on your dog.

Rat poison. Rat poison usually contains a powerful antico-
agulant that causes its victims to bleed to death. Dogs that
accidentally ingest this substance should be induced to vomit
immediately, to decrease the chances of the toxin's absorption.
They should also be treated with vitamin K injections (plus

supportive care as necessary) to boost the ability of their blood to clot.

Other rodenticidal products contain strychnine. This poison is rapidly absorbed, causing convulsions and death within a short time. Immediate induction of vomiting is helpful in the case of strychnine poisoning, but don't waste any time getting to a veterinarian.

Acids, alkalis and petroleum products. Vomiting is contraindicated in the case of these poisonings, so it's best to consult your veterinarian about specific treatment.

However, here are some general guidelines to help you buy time if assistance is not immediately available.

If the dog has ingested an acidic poison, administer an antacid such as milk of magnesia or Pepto-Bismol. Approximately two teaspoons per five pounds of body weight will help neutralize the acid. To neutralize an alkali substance, give the same dosage of a one part vinegar–four parts water mixture.

In the case of petroleum distillate poisoning, use mineral or vegetable oil to coat the gastrointestinal tract. The dose is one tablespoon per five pounds of body weight.

Antifreeze. Antifreeze, a potent poison thought to taste sweet, is very attractive to animals. Unfortunately, only a tiny amount needs to be ingested before serious kidney damage results. If you suspect that your dog has sampled some of this green liquid, immediately seek veterinary help. There are no measures to take at home.

Topical Irritants

Paint, tar or grease. Never try to remove paint, tar or grease from a dog's coat with turpentine, gasoline or other harsh chemicals. These remedies are extremely irritating to the skin and may cause severe reactions. Vegetable oil, on the other hand, works quite well in removing tar and grease from the coat. This may be followed by a cleansing bath using mild dishwashing detergent. The best way to remove paint is to simply (though carefully) cut it away.

Burns. Minor burns are best treated by carefully clipping the hair away from the affected area, cleaning if necessary with a mild soap and applying a topical antibiotic or steroid ointment. Extensive burns need immediate veterinary care.

Hot spots. Hot spots are focal skin infections that, although not associated with burns, actually feel warm to the touch. They are usually round, red, moist and painful. Dogs can't seem to stop licking and chewing at the area.

Clip hair away from hot spots, clean thoroughly and then treat with antibiotic or steroid ointment. If hot spots are severe dogs are often given oral antibiotics and forced to wear Elizabethan collars, plastic barriers which prevent the dog from reaching the hot spot with its mouth. Hot spots often look very minor at first, but explode into large problems if left unattended.

Dog Fights

Dog fights frequently result from the ignorance or indifference of the dogs' owners. Don't let your dog roam. It should be on leash at all times when outdoors and off your property. If a fight should occur, try to separate the dogs as best you can without placing yourself at risk; sometimes dousing them with water startles dogs enough to stop a fight. Remove other dogs from the vicinity to reduce the frenzy.

The wounds sustained in a dog fight may look minor, but they can quickly develop into major infections. Small puncture wounds are a misleading indication of the damage to muscle and other underlying tissues. Bite wounds must be thoroughly cleaned and flushed with something like hydrogen peroxide; often debridement and/or drains are necessary to effect a cure. Treatment may be prolonged and costly. Seek veterinary help immediately.

Convulsions

The best course of action to take with a dog undergoing a convulsion is to protect it from injuring itself by falling or striking its head against hard objects. A large blanket or towel may be placed under the dog's head and limbs. Take care when handling the head since the dog may accidentally bite you. There is no need to worry about the dog swallowing its tongue, so don't risk getting hurt by reaching into its mouth.

Seizures vary in length. They are rarely life threatening in themselves, but can be very serious if the dog is unable to come out of a convulsion or has multiple seizures with barely a break between them. See the veterinarian as soon as possible to try to determine the cause.

THE DOG'S EXTERNAL AND SKELETAL ANATOMY

ON THE SEVEN pages that follow we present a series of magnificent drawings by Mr. Stephen J. Hubbell, a celebrated artist and dog show judge. These clearly demonstrate what a wonderful work of design the dog's body truly is. Study these carefully and you will develop a deeper appreciation of your dog and its capacity to function so well in such an amazing variety of ways.

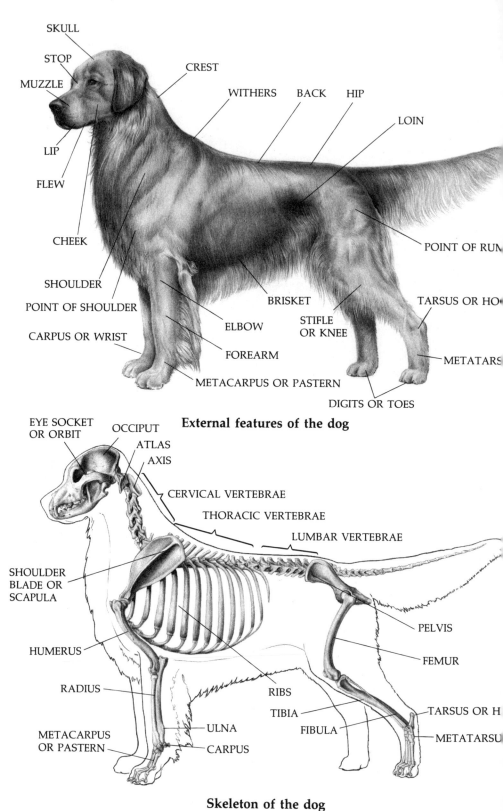

External features of the dog

SKULL

STOP

MUZZLE

CREST

WITHERS   BACK   HIP

LOIN

LIP

FLEW

POINT OF RUM

CHEEK

TARSUS OR HO

SHOULDER

POINT OF SHOULDER

BRISKET

STIFLE
OR KNEE

CARPUS OR WRIST

METATARS

ELBOW

FOREARM

METACARPUS OR PASTERN

DIGITS OR TOES

EYE SOCKET
OR ORBIT   OCCIPUT

ATLAS

AXIS

CERVICAL VERTEBRAE

THORACIC VERTEBRAE

LUMBAR VERTEBRAE

SHOULDER
BLADE OR
SCAPULA

PELVIS

HUMERUS

FEMUR

RADIUS

RIBS

TIBIA

TARSUS OR H

ULNA

FIBULA

METATARSU

METACARPUS
OR PASTERN

CARPUS

Skeleton of the dog

Drawings by Stephen J. Hubbell

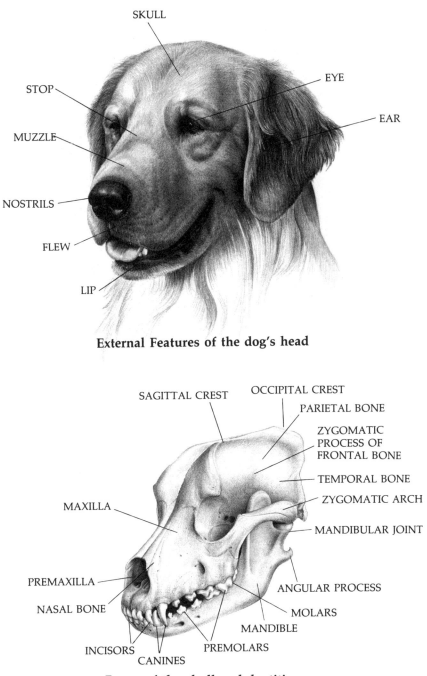

SKULL

STOP

MUZZLE

NOSTRILS

FLEW

LIP

EYE

EAR

External Features of the dog's head

SAGITTAL CREST

OCCIPITAL CREST

PARIETAL BONE

ZYGOMATIC PROCESS OF FRONTAL BONE

TEMPORAL BONE

ZYGOMATIC ARCH

MANDIBULAR JOINT

MAXILLA

PREMAXILLA

NASAL BONE

ANGULAR PROCESS

MOLARS

MANDIBLE

INCISORS

CANINES

PREMOLARS

Bones of the skull and dentition

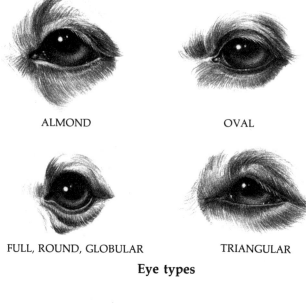

ALMOND

OVAL

FULL, ROUND, GLOBULAR

TRIANGULAR

Eye types

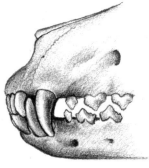

LEVEL

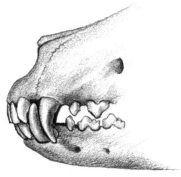

SCISSORS

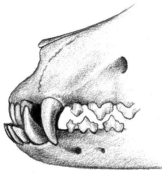

UNDERSHOT

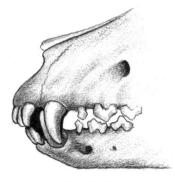

OVERSHOT

Bites

NORMAL, STRAIGHT

TOO NARROW IN FRONT
AND EAST-WEST FEET

CHIPPENDALE OR
FIDDLE FRONT

OUT AT ELBOW AND
TOO WIDE IN FRONT

STRAIGHT FRONT   KNUCKLED OVER   DOWN IN PASTERN

PADS

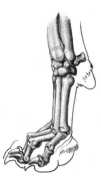

BONES OF THE FOOT

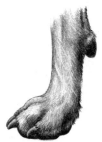

ROUND OR CAT FOOT

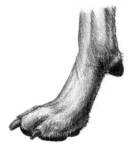

HARE FOOT

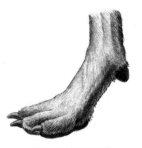

FLAT FOOT OR
DOWN IN PASTERN

SPLAY FOOT

Feet

CORRECT, STRAIGHT, NORMAL

COW-HOCKED

BANDY OR WIDE

NARROW

NORMAL ANGULATED
HINDQUARTERS

STRAIGHT STIFLES

Rears

PLUME

GAY

CURLED

DOUBLE CURL

SICKLE

OTTER

WHIP

RING AT END

SNAP

SCREW

Tails

APPENDIX I: CLUBS

No matter what your interest in dogs, the chances are good that there's a dog club near you where you can meet people who share your interests. Believe it or not, at latest count in early 1991, there were more than *3,950* different dog clubs in the United States which are holding events under AKC *Rules* and *Regulations.* So the odds are there's a club near you.

AKC recognizes eight different types of clubs: All-breed clubs, specialty (breed) clubs, obedience clubs, tracking clubs, field trial clubs, hunting test clubs, herding clubs, and coonhound clubs.

The largest group of clubs is the specialty or breed clubs. There are more than 1,700 specialty clubs in the United States. There are two types of specialty clubs. The first is the national (or parent) breed club—an example would be the Golden Retriever Club of America. AKC only recognizes one club as the national or parent breed club for each recognized breed. The second type of specialty (breed) club is the local specialty; for example, the Golden Retriever Club of Greater Los Angeles or the Kansas City Golden Retriever Club.

It is this extensive network of serious fanciers of the respective breeds that you should be contacting to help you choose your dog. You may obtain detailed information about the clubs nearest you by contacting AKC Customer Service, 580 Centerview Drive, Raleigh, North Carolina 27606, phone number *919-233-9767.*

APPENDIX II: TITLES

Dogs compete in the various competitions offered under the *Rules* and *Regulations* of the American Kennel Club for twenty different titles. When a dog completes the requirements for one of the titles, official note of the title is made on the dog's AKC records. Thereafter the notation of title will always appear with the dog's name in AKC's records. Seven of the titles are indicated before the dog's name (prefixes), and thirteen appear after the dog's name (suffixes). The titles and their abbreviations are:

Prefixes:
	CH	Champion
	FC	Field Champion
	AFC	Amateur Field Champion
	OTCH	Obedience Trial Champion
	HCH	Herding Champion
	DC	Dual Champion (CH & FC)
	TC	Triple Champion (CH, FC, & OTCH)

Suffixes:
	CD	Companion Dog
	CDX	Companion Dog Excellent
	UD	Utility Dog
	TD	Tracking Dog
	TDX	Tracking Dog Excellent

JH	Junior Hunter
SH	Senior Hunter
MH	Master Hunter
HT	Herding Tested
PT	Pre-trial Tested
HS	Herding Started
HI	Herding Intermediate
HX	Herding Excellent

GLOSSARY

Abdomen: The portion of the dog's body between the chest and the hindquarters.

Action: Any performance of function or movement, either of any part or organ, or of the whole body. Used as a synonym for gait in some standards.

AKC: American Kennel Club.

Albino: Animal deficient in pigmentation.

Almond eyes: The eye set in surrounding tissue of almond shape.

Angulation: The angles formed by a meeting of the bones; mainly, the shoulder, upper arm, stifle, and hock.

Arm: The anatomical region between the shoulder and elbow joints, consisting of the humerus and associated muscles. Sometimes referred to as "upper arm."

Back: Variable in meaning depending upon context of the standard. In some standards defined as the vertebrae between the withers and the loin.

Bad mouth: Crooked or unaligned teeth; bite over or undershot in excess of standard specifications.

Balanced: A consistent whole; symmetrical, typically proportioned as a whole or as regards its separate parts; i.e., balance of head, balance of body, or balance of head and body.

Bandy legs: Having a bend of leg outward.

Barrel: Rounded rib section.

Bay: The prolonged bark or voice of the hunting hound.

Beady eyes: Small, round and glittering, imparting an expression foreign to the breed.

Beard: Thick, long hair growth on the underjaw.

Beefy: Overheavy development of the hindquarters.

Belly: The underline of the abdomen.

Bench show: A dog show at which the dogs competing for prizes are "benched" or leashed on benches.

Best in show: A dog-show award to the dog adjudged best of all breeds.

Bird dog: A sporting dog trained to hunt birds.

Bitch: A female dog.

Bite: The relative position of the upper and lower teeth when the mouth is closed. *See* Level bite, Scissors bite, Undershot, Overshot.

Blaze: A white stripe running up the center of the face usually between the eyes.

Blocky: Square or cubelike formation of the head.

Bloom: The sheen of a coat in prime condition.

Board: To feed, house, and care for a dog for a fee.

Bodied up: Mature, well-developed.

Body: The anatomical section between the forequarters and the hindquarters.

Body length: Distance from the point of the shoulder to the rearmost projection of the upper thigh (point of the buttocks).

Bone: The relative size (girth) of a dog's leg bones. Substance.

Bossy: Overdevelopment of the shoulder muscles.

Break: Term used to describe changing of coat color from puppies to adult stages.

Breastbone: Bone in forepart of chest.

Breed: Pure-bred dogs more or less uniform in size and structure, as produced and maintained by man.

Breeder: A person who breeds dogs. Under AKC rules the breeder of a dog is the owner (or, if the dam was leased, the lessee) of the dam of the dog when the dam was bred.

Breeding particulars: Sire, dam, date of birth, sex, color, etc.

Brick-shaped: Rectangular.

Brindle: A fine even mixture of black hairs with hairs of a lighter color, usually tan, brown, or gray.

Brisket: The forepart of the body below the chest, between the forelegs, closest to the ribs.

Broken color: Self color broken by white or another color.

Broken-haired: A roughed-up wire coat.

Broken-up face: A receding nose, together with a deep stop, wrinkle, and undershot jaw. (Bulldog, Pekingese.)

Brood bitch: A female used for breeding. Brood matron.

Brows: The ridges formed above the eyes by frontal bone contours. (Superciliary arches.)

Brush: A bushy tail; a tail heavy with hair.

Brushing: A gaiting fault, when parallel pasterns are so close that the legs "brush" in passing.

Bull neck: A heavy neck, well-muscled.

Burr: The inside of the ear; i.e., the irregular formation visible within the cup.

Butterfly nose: A parti-colored nose; i.e., dark, spotted with flesh color.

Buttocks: The rump or hips.

Button ear: The ear flap folding forward, the tip lying close to the skull so as to cover the orifice, and pointing toward the eye.

Camel back: Arched back, like that of one-hump camel.

Canine: A group of animals—dogs, foxes, wolves, jackals.

Canines: The two upper and two lower sharp-pointed teeth next to the incisors. Fangs.

Cape: Profuse hair enveloping the shoulder region.

Carpals: Bones of the pastern joints.

Castrate: To remove the testicles of the male dog.

Cat foot: Round, compact foot, with well-arched toes, tightly bunched or close-cupped.

CD (Companion Dog): A suffix used with the name of a dog that has been recorded a Companion Dog by AKC as a result of having won certain minimum scores in Novice Classes at a specified number of AKC licensed or member obedience trials.

CDX (Companion Dog Excellent): A suffix used with the name of a dog that has been recorded a Companion Dog Excellent by AKC as a result of having won certain minimum scores in Open Classes at a specified number of AKC licensed or member obedience trials.

Champion (Ch.): A prefix used with the name of a dog that has been recorded a Champion by AKC as a result of defeating a specified number of dogs in specified competition at a series of AKC licensed or member dog shows.

Character: Expression, individuality, and general appearance and deportment as considered typical of a breed.

Cheeky: Cheeks prominently rounded; thick, protruding.

Chest: The part of the body or trunk that is enclosed by the ribs.

China eye: A clear blue eye.

Chippendale front: Named after the Chippendale chair. Forelegs out at elbows, pasterns close, and feet turned out. *See:* Fiddle front, French front.

Chiseled: Clean-cut in head, particularly beneath the eyes.

Choke collar: A leather or chain collar fitted to the dog's neck in such a manner that the degree of tension exerted by the hand tightens or loosens it.

Chops: Jowls or pendulous flesh of the lips and jaw. (Bulldog.)

Chorea: A nervous jerking caused by involuntary contraction of the muscles, usually affecting the face or legs.

Clip: The method of trimming the coat in some breeds, notably the Poodle.

Clipping: When pertaining to gait, the back foot striking the front foot.

Cloddy: Low, thickset, comparatively heavy.

Close-coupled: Comparatively short from withers to hipbones.

Coarse: Lacking refinement.

Coat: The dog's hair covering. Most breeds possess two coats, an outer coat and an undercoat.

Cobby: Short-bodied, compact.

Collar: The marking around the neck, usually white. Also a leather or chain for restraining or leading the dog, when the leash is attached.

Compact: Term used to describe the firmly joined union of various body parts. Also to describe a short to medium length coat, very close-lying, with a dense undercoat and giving a smooth outline.

Condition: Health as shown by the coat, state of flesh, general appearance and deportment.

Conformation: The form and structure, make and shape; arrangement of the parts in conformance with breed-standard demands.

Congenital: An inherited feature present at birth.

Coupling: The part of the body between the ribs and pelvis; the loin.

Covering ground: The ratio of the distance between the ground and brisket and the distance between front and rear legs. As in "covers too much ground."

Cow-hocked: When the hocks turn toward each other.

Crank tail: A tail carried down and resembling a crank in shape.

Crest: The upper, arched portion of the neck.

Cropping: The cutting or trimming of the ear leather for the purpose of inducing the ears to stand erect.

Crossbred: A dog whose sire and dam are representatives of two different breeds.

Croup: The back part of the back, above the hind legs.

Crown: The highest part of the head: the topskull.

Cryptorchid: The adult whose testicles are abnormally retained in the abdominal cavity. Bilateral cryptorchidism involves both sides; that is, neither testicle has descended into the scrotum. Unilateral cryptorchidism involves one side only; that is, one testicle is retained or hidden, and one descended.

Cur: A mongrel.

Cushion: Fullness or thickness of the upper lips.

Cynology: The study of canines.

Dam: The female parent.

Deciduous: Not permanent, but cast off at maturity. Used in reference to baby or milk teeth.

Dentition: Reference to the number of teeth characteristic of a species, and to their arrangement in the jaws.

Depth of chest: Measured from the withers to the lowest point of the sternum.

Dewclaw: An extra claw or functionless digit on the inside of the leg; a rudimentary fifth toe.

Dewlap: Loose, pendulous skin under the throat.

Disqualification: A decision made by a judge or by a bench show committee following a determination that a dog has a condition that makes it ineligible for any further competition under the dog show rules or under the standard for its breed.

Distemper teeth: Teeth discolored or pitted as a result of distemper or other enervating disease or deficiency.

Dock: To shorten the tail by cutting.

Dog: A male dog; also used collectively to designate both male and female.

Dog show: A competitive exhibition for dogs at which the dogs are judged in accordance with an established standard of perfection for each breed.

Dog Show, Conformation (Licensed): An event held under AKC rules at which championship points are awarded. May be for *all breeds,* or for a single breed (Specialty Show).

Domed: Evenly rounded in topskull; convex instead of flat. Domy.

Double coat: An outer coat resistant to weather and protective against brush and brambles, together with an undercoat of softer hair for warmth and water-proofing.

Down-faced: The muzzle inclining downwards from the skull to the tip of the nose.

Down in pastern: Weak or faulty pastern (metacarpus) set at a pronounced angle from the vertical.

Drive: A solid thrusting of the hindquarters, denoting sound locomotion.

Drop ear: The ends of the ear folded or drooping forward, as contrasted with erect or prick ears.

Dry neck: The skin taut; neither loose nor wrinkled.

Dual champion: A dog that has won both a bench show and a field trial championship.

Dudley nose: Flesh-colored.

East-West front: Incorrectly positioned pasterns that cause the feet to turn outwards. Usually associated with a narrow front.

Elbow: The joint between the upper arm and the forearm.

Elbows out: Turning out or off from the body; not held close.

Entire: A dog whose reproductive system is complete.

Even bite: Meeting of front teeth at edges with no overlap of upper or lower teeth.

Ewe neck: Concave curvature of the top neckline.

Expression: The general appearance of all features of the head as viewed from the front and as typical of the breed.

Eyeteeth: The upper canines.

Fall: Hair overhanging the face.

Fallow: Pale cream to light fawn color; pale; pale yellow; yellow-red.

Fancier: A person especially interested and usually active in some phase of the sport of pure-bred dogs.

Fangs: *See* Canines.

Fawn: A brown, red-yellow with hue of medium brilliance.

Femur: Thigh bone. Extends from hip to stifle.

Fetch: The retrieve of game by the dog; also the command to do so.

Fibula: The outer and smaller of the two bones of the lower thigh.

Fiddle front: Forelegs out at elbows, pasterns close, and feet turned out. French front.

Field Champion (Field Ch.): A prefix used with the name of a dog that has been recorded a Field Champion by AKC as a result of defeating a specified number of dogs in specified competition at a series of AKC licensed or member field trials.

Field trial: A competition for certain Hound or Sporting Breeds in which dogs are judged on ability and style in finding or retrieving game or following a game trail.

Filled-up face: Smooth facial contours, free of excessive muscular development.

Flag: A long tail carried high; usually referring to one of the Pointing Breeds.

Flank: The side of the body between the last rib and the hip.

Flat bone: The leg bone whose girth is elliptical rather than round.

Flat-sided: Ribs insufficiently rounded as they approach the sternum or breast-bone.

Flat withers: A fault that is the result of short upright shoulder blades that unattractively join the withers abruptly.

Flews: Upper lips pendulous, particularly at their inner corners.

Floating rib: The last, or 13th rib, which is unattached to other ribs.

Flush: To drive birds from cover, to force them to take flight. To spring.

Flying ears: Any characteristic drop ears or semi-prick ears that stand or "fly."

Forearm: The bone of the forelegs between the elbow and the pastern.

Foreface: The front part of the head, before the eyes. Muzzle.

Forequarters: The combined front assembly from its uppermost component, the shoulder blade, down to the feet.

Foster mother: A bitch or other animal, such as a cat, used to nurse whelps not her own.

Foxy: Sharp expression; pointed nose with short foreface.

French front: *See* Fiddle front.

Front: The forepart of the body as viewed head on; i.e., forelegs, chest, brisket, and shoulder line.

Frontal bone: The skull bone over the eyes.

Furnishings: The long hair on the foreface of certain breeds.

Furrow: A slight indentation or median line down the center of the skull to the stop.

Gait: The pattern of footsteps at various rates of speed, each pattern distinguished by a particular rhythm and footfall. The two gaits acceptable in the show ring are walk and trot.

Gay tail: The tail carried up.

Genealogy: Recorded family descent.

Goose neck: An elongated, tubular-shaped neck. Also termed swan neck.

Goose rump: Too steep or sloping a croup.

Grizzle: Bluish-gray color.

Groom: To brush, comb, trim, or otherwise make a dog's coat neat.

Groups: The breeds as grouped in seven divisions to facilitate judging.

Guard hairs: The longer, smoother, stiffer hairs which grow through the undercoat and normally conceal it.

Gun dog: A dog trained to work with its master in finding live game and retrieving game that has been shot.

Hackles: Hair on neck and back raised involuntarily in fright or anger.

Hallmark: A distinguishing characteristic, such as the spectacles of the Keeshond.

Ham: Muscular development of the hind leg just above the stifle.

Handler: A person who handles a dog in the show ring or at a field trial.

Hare foot: Foot in which the two center digits appear appreciably longer than the outside and inside toes of the foot, and the arching of the toes is less marked, making the foot appear longer overall.

Harness: A leather strap shaped around the shoulders and chest, with a ring at its top over the withers.

Haw: A third eyelid or membrane in the inside corner of the eye.

Head planes: Viewed in profile, the contours of the top skull from occiput to stop, and of the foreface from stop to tip of nose. Usually spoken of in relation to one another.

Heat: Seasonal period of the female. Estrus.

Heel: *See* Hock; also a command to the dog to keep close beside its handler.

Height: Vertical measurement from the withers to the ground; referred to usually as shoulder height. *See* Withers.

High standing: Tall and upstanding, with plenty of leg.

Hindquarters: Rear assembly of dog (pelvis, thighs, hocks and paws).

Hock: The tarsus or collection of bones of the hind leg forming the joint between the second thigh and the metatarsus; the dog's true heel.

Hocks well let down: Hock joints close to the ground.

Hound: A dog commonly used for hunting by scent or sight.

Hound-marked: A coloration composed of white, tan, and black. The ground color, usually white, may be marked with tan and/or black patches on the head, back, legs, and tail. The extent and the exact location of such markings, however, differ in breeds and individuals.

Inbreeding: The mating of closely related dogs of the same standard breed.

Incisors: The six upper and six lower front teeth between the canines. Their point of contact forms the "bite."

In-shoulder: Shoulders point in, not parallel with backbone, a fault found in dogs with shoulder blades too far forward on chest.

Interbreeding: The breeding together of dogs of different breeds.

Iris: The colored membrane surrounding the pupil of the eye.

Isabella: Fawn or light bay color.

Jowls: Flesh of lips and jaws.

Judge: The arbiter in the dog show ring, obedience trial, or field trial.

Keel: The rounded outline of the lower chest, between the prosternum and end of the breastbone.

Kennel: Building or enclosure where dogs are kept.

Kink tail: The tail sharply bent.

Kiss marks: Tan spots on the cheeks and over the eyes.

Knee joint: Stifle joint.

Knuckling over: Faulty structure of carpus (wrist) joint allowing it to double forward under the weight of the standing dog; double-jointed wrist, often with slight swelling of the bones.

Layback: The angle of the shoulder blade as compared with the vertical.

Lead: A strap, cord, or chain attached to the collar or harness for the purpose of restraining or leading the dog. Leash.

Leather: The flap of the ear.

Level bite: When the front teeth (incisors) of the upper and lower jaws meet exactly edge to edge. Pincer bite.

Level gait: Dog moves without rise or fall of withers.

Line breeding: The mating of related dogs of the same standard breed, within the line or family, to a common ancestor, as, for example, a dog to his grand-dam or a bitch to her grandsire.

Lippy: Pendulous lips or lips that do not fit tightly.

Litter: The puppy or puppies of one whelping.

Liver: A color; i.e., deep, reddish brown.

Loaded shoulders: When the shoulder blades are shoved out from the body by overdevelopment of the muscles.

Loin: Region of the body on either side of the vertebral column between the last ribs and the hindquarters.

Loose slung: Construction in which the attachment of the body at the shoulders is looser than desirable.

Lower thigh: *See* Second thigh.

Lumber: Superfluous flesh.

Lumbering: An awkward gait.

Mane: Long and profuse hair on top and sides of the neck.

Mask: Dark shading on the foreface. (Mastiff, Boxer, Pekingese.)

Match show: Usually an informal dog show at which no championship points are awarded.

Mate: To breed a dog and bitch.

Median line: *See* Furrow.

Metatarsus: Rear pastern.

Milk teeth: First teeth.

Miscellaneous Class: A competitive class at dog shows for dogs of certain specified breeds for which no regular dog show classification is provided.

Mismarks: Self colors with any area of white on back between withers and tail, on sides between elbows and back of hindquarters, or on ears. Black with white markings and no tan present. (Pembroke Welsh Corgi.)

Molars: Dog has four premolars on each side of the upper and lower jar. There are two true molars on each side of the upper jaw, and three on each side of the lower jaw. Upper molars have three roots, lower have two roots.

Molera: Incomplete, imperfect or abnormal ossification of the skull.

Mongrel: A dog whose parents are of two different breeds.

Monorchid: A unilateral cryptorchid. *See* Cryptorchid.

Moving close: When the hocks turn in and pasterns drop straight to the ground and move parallel to one another, the dog is "moving close" in the rear. Action places severe strain on ligaments and muscles.

Moving straight: Term descriptive of balanced gaiting in which angle of inclination begins at the shoulder, or hip joint, and limbs remain relatively straight from these points to the pads of the feet, even as the legs flex or extend in reaching or thrusting.

Muzzle: The head in front of the eyes—nasal bone, nostrils, and jaws. Foreface. Also, a strap or wire cage attached to the foreface to prevent the dog from biting or from picking up food.

Muzzle band: White marking around the muzzle.

Neck well set-on: Good neckline, merging gradually with strong withers, forming a pleasing transition into topline.

Nick: A breeding that produces desirable puppies.

Nose: Organ of smell; also, the ability to detect by means of scent.

Obedience Trial (Licensed): An event held under AKC rules at which a "leg" toward an obedience degree can be earned.

Obedience Trial Champion (OTCH): A prefix used with the name of a dog that has been recorded an Obedience Trial Champion by the AKC as the result of having won the number of points and First Place wins specified in the current Obedience Regulations.

Obliquely placed eyes: Eyes with outer corners higher up in the skull than their inner ones. Requested in Alaskan Malamute and Bull Terrier standards.

Oblique shoulders: Shoulders well laid back. The ideal shoulder should slant at 45 degrees to the ground, forming an approximate right angle with the humerus at the shoulder joint.

Occiput: Upper, back point of the skull.

Occipital protuberance: A prominently raised occiput characteristic of some gun-dog breeds.

Open bitch: A bitch that can be bred.

Open Class: A class at dog shows in which all dogs of a breed, champions and imported dogs included, may compete.

Otter tail: Thick at the root, round, and tapering, with the hair parted or divided on the underside.

Out at elbows: Elbows turning out from the body as opposed to being held close.

Out at shoulder: With shoulder blades loosely attached to the body, leaving the shoulders jutting out in relief and increasing the breadth of the front.

Out at walk: To lease or lend a puppy to someone for raising.

Outcrossing: The mating of unrelated individuals of the same breed.

Oval chest: Chest deeper than wide.

Overhang: A heavy or pronounced brow. (Pekingese.)

Overreaching: Fault in the trot caused by more angulation and drive from behind than in front, so that the rear feet are forced to step to one side of the forefeet to avoid interfering or clipping.

Overshot: The front teeth (incisors) of the upper jaw overlap and do not touch the front teeth of the lower jaw when the mouth is closed.

Pads: Tough, shock-absorbing projections on the underside of the feet. Soles.

Paper foot: A flat foot with thin pads.

Parent club: National club for the breed. Listing with name and address of secretary can be obtained from American Kennel Club, 51 Madison Avenue, New York, N.Y. 10010.

Parti-color: Variegated in patches of two or more colors.

Pastern: Commonly recognized as the region of the foreleg between the carpus or wrist and the digits.

Pedigree: The written record of a dog's descent of three generations or more.

Pelvis: Hip bone.

Pied: Comparatively large patches of two or more colors. Piebald, parti-colored.

Pigeon-breast: A chest with a short protruding breastbone.

Pigeon-toed: Toes pointing in.

Pig Eyes: Eyes set too close.

Pile: Dense undercoat of soft hair.

Plume: A long fringe of hair hanging from the tail as in Setters.

Point: The immovable stance of the hunting dog taken to indicate the presence and position of game.

Points: Color on face, ears, legs, and tail when correlated—usually white, black or tan.

Police dog: Any dog trained for police work.

Prick ear: Carried erect and usually pointed at the tip.

Professional handler: A person who shows dogs for a fee.

Pump handle: Long tail, carried high.

Puppy: A dog under twelve months of age.

Pure-bred: A dog whose sire and dam belong to the same breed, and are themselves of unmixed descent since recognition of the breed.

Quality: Refinement, fineness.

Racy: Tall, of comparatively slight build.

Rangy: Long-bodied, usually lacking depth in chest.

Rat tail: The root thick and covered with soft curls; at the tip devoid of hair, or having the appearance of being clipped.

Reach of front: Length of forward stride taken by forelegs without wasted or excessive motion.

Register: To record with the AKC a dog's breeding particulars.

Retrieve: A hunting term. The act of bringing back shot game to the handler.

Ribbed up: Long ribs that angle back from the spinal column (45 degrees is ideal); last rib is long.

Ring tail: Carried up and around almost in a circle.

Roach back: A convex curvature of the back toward the loin.

Rocking horse: Both front and rear legs extended out from body as in old-fashioned rocking horse.

Roman nose: A nose whose bridge is so comparatively high as to form a slightly convex line from forehead to nose tip. Ram's nose.

Rose ear: A small drop ear which folds over and back so as to reveal the burr.

Rudder: The tail.

Ruff: Thick, longer hair growth around the neck.

Saber tail: Carried in a semi-circle.

Sable: A lacing of black hairs over a lighter ground color. In Collies and Shetland Sheepdogs, a brown color ranging from golden to mahogany.

Saddle back: Overlong back, with a dip behind the withers.

Scissors bite: A bite in which the outer side of the lower incisors touches the inner side of the upper incisors.

Screw tail: A naturally short tail twisted in more or less spiral formation.

Second thigh: That part of the hindquarter from the stifle to the hock, corresponding to the human shin and calf. Lower thigh.

Self color: One color or whole color except for lighter shadings.

Seeing Eye dog: A dog trained as a guide for the blind.

Semi-prick ears: Ears carried erect with just the tips leaning forward.

Septum: The line extending vertically between the nostrils.

Shelly: A shallow, narrow body, lacking the correct amount of bone.

Short back: A back shorter than the height at the withers, or one short in relation to specific breed requirements.

Shoulder-height: Height of dog's body as measured from the withers to the ground. *See* Withers.

Sickle hocked: Inability to straighten the hock joint on the back reach of the hind leg.

Sickle tail: Carried out and up in a semicircle.

Sire: The male parent.

Skully: Thick and coarse through skull.

Slab sided: Flat ribs with too little spring from spinal column.

Sled dogs: Dogs worked usually in teams to draw sleds.

Sloping shoulder: The shoulder blade set obliquely or "laid back."

Smooth coat: Short hair, close-lying.

Snipy: A pointed, weak muzzle.

Snow nose: Nose normally solid black, but acquires pink streak in winter. (Specified as acceptable in Siberian Husky standard.)

Soundness: The state of mental and physical health when all organs and faculties are complete and functioning normally, each in its rightful relation to the other.

Spay: To perform a surgical operation on the bitch's reproductive organs to prevent conception.

Spectacles: Shadings or dark markings over or around the eyes or from eyes to ears.

Spike tail: Straight short tail that tapers rapidly along its length.

Splashed: Irregularly patched, color on white or white on color.

Splayfoot: A flat foot with toes spreading. Open foot, open-toed.

Spread: Width between the forelegs when accentuated.

Spread hocks: Hocks pointing outward.

Spring of ribs: Curvature of ribs for heart and lung capacity.

Square body: A dog whose measurements from withers to the ground equals that from point of shoulder to the rearmost projection of the upper thigh.

Squirrel tail: Carried up and curving more or less forward.

Stance: Manner of standing.

Standard: A description of the ideal dog of each recognized breed, to serve as a word pattern by which dogs are judged at shows.

Standoff coat: A long or heavy coat that stands off from the body.

Staring coat: The hair dry, harsh, and sometimes curling at the tips.

Station: Comparative height from the ground, as high-stationed, low-stationed.

Steep: Used to denote insufficiently acute angles of articulation. For example, a steep front describes a more upright shoulder placement than is perferred.

Stern: Tail of a sporting dog or hound.

Sternum: Breastbone.

Stifle: The joint of the hind leg between the thigh and the second thigh. The dog's knee.

Stop: The step up from muzzle to skull; indentation between the eyes where the nasal bone and skull meet.

Straight-hocked: Lacking appreciable angulation at the hock joints. Straight behind.

Straight in pastern: Little or no bend between joint and foot.

Straight shoulders: The shoulder blades rather straight up and down, as opposed to sloping or "well laid back."

Stud book: A record of the breeding particulars of dogs of recognized breeds.

Stud dog: A male dog used for breeding purposes.

Substance: Bone.

Superciliary arches: The ridge, projection, or prominence of the frontal bone of the skull over the eye; the brow.

Swayback: Concave curvature of the back line between the withers and the hipbones.

Symmetry: Pleasing balance between all parts of the dog.

Tail set: How the base of the tail sets on the rump.

TD (Tracking Dog): A suffix used with the name of a dog that has been recorded a Tracking Dog as a result of having passed an AKC licensed or member tracking test. The title may be combined with the UD title and shown as UDT.

TDX (Tracking Dog Excellent): A suffix used with the name of a dog that has been recorded a Tracking Dog Excellent as a result of having passed an AKC licensed or member tracking dog excellent test. The title may be combined with the UDT title and shown as UDTX.

Terrier: A group of dogs used originally for hunting vermin.

Terrier front: Straight front, as found on Fox Terriers.

Testicles: The male gonad, gland which produces spermatozoa. AKC regulations specify that a male which does not have two normal testicles normally located in the scrotum may not compete at any show and will be disqualified, except that a castrated male may be entered in obedience trials, tracking tests, field trials (except Beagles) and as Stud Dog in a Stud Dog class.

Thigh: The hindquarter from hip to stifle.

Throatiness: An excess of loose skin under the throat.

Thumb marks: Black spots on the region of the pastern.

Ticked: Small, isolated areas of black or colored hairs on a white ground.

Topknot: A tuft of longer hair on top of the head.

Topline: The dog's outline from just behind the withers to the tail set.

Toy dog: One of a group of dogs characterized by very small size.

Triangular eye: The eye set in surrounding tissue of triangular shape; three-cornered eye.

Tri-color: Three-color; white, black, and tan.

Trim: To groom the coat by plucking or clipping.

Triple Champion: A dog that has won bench show, field trial and obedience trial championships.

Trot: A rhythmic two-beat diagonal gait in which the feet at diagonally opposite ends of the body strike the ground together; i.e., right hind with left front and left hind with right front.

Tuck-up: Characterized by markedly shallower body depth at the loin. Small-waisted.

Tulip ear: Ears carried with a slight forward curvature.

Turn-up: An uptilted foreface.

Type: The characteristic qualities distinguishing a breed; the embodiment of a standard's essentials.

UD (Utility Dog): A suffix used with the name of a dog that has been recorded a Utility Dog by AKC as a result of having won certain minimum scores in Utility Classes at a specified number of AKC licensed or member obedience trials. The title may be combined with TD or TDX title and shown as UDT or UDTX.

Underline: The combined contours of the brisket and the abdominal floor.

Undershot: The front teeth (incisors) of the lower jaw overlapping or projecting beyond the front teeth of the upper jaw when the mouth is closed.

Unsound: A dog incapable of performing the functions for which it was designed.

Upper arm: The humerus or bone of the foreleg, between the shoulder blade and the forearm.

Veil: The portion of the dog's forelock hanging straight down over the eyes, or partially covering them.

Vent: The anal opening.

Walk: Gaiting pattern in which three legs are in support of the body at all times, each foot lifting from the ground one at a time in regular sequence.

Walleye: An eye with a whitish iris; a blue eye, fisheye, pearl eye.

Webbed: Connected by a membrane. Webbed feet are important for water-retrieving breeds. (See Chesapeake Bay Retriever and Newfoundland standards.)

Weedy: An insufficient amount of bone; light-boned.

Well let down: Having short hocks.

Wet neck: Loose or superfluous skin; with dewlap.

Wheaten: Pale yellow or fawn color.

Wheel back: The back line arched markedly over the loin. Roached.

Whip tail: Carried out stiffly straight, and pointed.

Whisker: Longer hairs on muzzle sides and underjaw.

Winners: An award given at dog shows to the best dog (Winners Dog) and best bitch (Winners Bitch) competing in regular classes.

Wirehair: A coat of hard, crisp, wiry texture.

Withers: The highest point of the shoulders, immediately behind the neck.

Wrinkle: Loose, folding skin on forehead and foreface.

Wry mouth: Lower jaw does not line up with upper jaw.

BIBLIOGRAPHY

The following bibliography includes books contained in the AKC library that are currently in print. Included are subjects of general interest as well as for the 25 breeds with the highest registration numbers for 1990.

DOGS

American Kennel Club. *The Complete Dog Book.* 17th ed. New York: Howell Book House, 1985.

Caras, Roger A., ed. *Harper's Illustrated Handbook of Dogs.* New York: Harper & Row Publishers, Inc., 1985.

Hancock, Judith M. *Friendship: You and Your Dog.* New York: Dutton, 1986.

Lowell, Michele. *Your Purebred Puppy: A Buyer's Guide.* 1st ed. New York: Henry Holt & Co., 1990.

Miller, Harry. *Common Sense Book of Puppy and Dog Care.* New York: Bantam, 1987.

Ruckert, Janet. *Are You My Dog? How to Find Your Best Friend.* Berkeley: Ten Speed Press, 1989.

Taylor, David. *The Ultimate Dog Book.* New York: Simon & Schuster, 1990.

Tortora, Daniel F. *The Right Dog For You.* New York: Simon & Schuster, 1980.

Walkowicz, Chris, and Bonnie Wilcox. *Atlas of Dog Breeds of the World.* 2nd ed. Neptune City, NJ: T.F.H. Publications, Inc., 1990.

DOGS—BREEDING

Cavill, David. *All About Mating, Whelping and Weaning.* London: Pelham Books Ltd., 1981.

Franklin J, Eleanor. *Practical Dog Breeding and Genetics.* London: Century Hutchinson Ltd., 1987.

Holst, Phyllis A. *Canine Reproduction: A Breeder's Guide.* Loveland, CO: Alpine Publications Inc., 1985.

Lee, Muriel P. *The Whelping and Rearing of Puppies: A Complete and Practical Guide.* Minneapolis: Plantin Press, 1984.

Portman-Graham, R. *The Mating and Whelping of Dogs.* 12th ed. London: Century Hutchinson Ltd., 1986.

Richards, Herbert. *Dog Breeding for Professionals.* Neptune City, NJ: T.F.H. Publications, Inc., 1978.

Robinson, Roy. *Genetics for Dog Breeders.* 2nd ed. New York: Pergamon Press, Inc., 1990.

Seranne, Anne. *The Joy of Breeding Your Own Show Dog.* New York: Howell Book House, 1980.

DOGS—CARE

Anderson, Robert. *Caring for Older Cats and Dogs: Extending Your Pet's Healthy Life.* Charlotte, VT: Williamson Publishing Co., 1990.

Animal Medical Center. *The Complete Book of Dog Health.* New York: Howell Book House, 1985.

Bower, John, and David Youngs. *The Health of Your Dog.* Alpine, CO: Alpine Publications Inc., 1989.

Carlson, Delbert G., and James M. Griffin. *Dog Owner's Home Veterinary Handbook.* New York: Howell Book House, 1980.

Delmar, Diana, and Peter Lawson. *The Guilt-Free Dog Owner's Guide: Caring for A Dog When You're Short on Time and Space.* Pownal, VT: Storey Publishing, 1990.

Edgson, F. Andrew. *First Aid and Nursing for Your Dog.* London: Century Hutchinson Ltd, 1987.

Gerstenfeld, Sheldon L. *The Dog Care Book.* Reading, MA: Addison-Wesley Publishing Co., Inc., 1989.

James, Ruth B. *The Dog Repair Book: A Do-It-Yourself Guide for the Dog Owner.* Mills, WY: Alpine Press, 1990.

Klever, Ulrich. *The Complete Book of Dog Care: How to Raise a Happy and Healthy Dog.* New York: Barron's, 1989.

Whitney, Leon F. and George D. *The Complete Book of Dog Care.* Rev. ed. Garden City, NY: Doubleday, 1985.

DOGS—FOOD

Cusick, William. *Canine Nutrition and Choosing the Best Food for Your Breed of Dog.* 1st ed. Aloha, OR: Adele Publications, Inc., 1990.

McDonald, Linda. *Bones to Biscuits: The Dog Foodbook.* Pasadena: Oaklawn Press, 1977.

DOGS—GROOMING

Fenger, Diane and Arlene F. Steinle. *The Standard Book of Dog Grooming.* Rev. ed. Fairfax, VA: Denlinger's Publishers, Ltd., 1983.

Hogg, Peggy A. *Grooming and Showing Toy Dogs.* Fairfax, VA: Denlinger's Publishers, Ltd., 1976.

Kalstone, Shirlee. *The Kalstone Guide to Grooming All Toy Dogs.* New York: Howell Book House, 1980.

Pinney, Christopher. *Guide to Home Pet Grooming.* New York: Barron's, 1990.

Stone, Ben and Pearl. *The Stone Guide to Dog Grooming for All Breeds.* New York: Howell Book House, 1981.

DOGS—PSYCHOLOGY

Fogle, Bruce. *The Dog's Mind.* New York: Penguin Books Ltd., 1990.

Milani, Myrna M. *The Body Language and Emotions of Dogs.* New York: William Morrow and Co., Inc., 1986.

Whitney, Leon F. *Dog Psychology—The Basis of Dog Training.* 2nd ed. New York: Howell Book House, 1971.

DOGS—TRAINING

Bauman, Diane. *Beyond Basic Dog Training.* New York: Howell Book House, 1986.

Benjamin, Carol L. *Dog Training for Kids.* Rev. ed. New York: Howell Book House, 1988.

Evans, Job M. *The Evans Guide for Housetraining Your Dog.* New York: Howell Book House, 1987.

Fox, Michael. *Superdog: Raising the Perfect Canine Companion.* New York: Howell Book House, 1990.

Holmes, John. *The Family Dog: Its Choice and Training.* N. Pomfret, VT: David & Charles, 1988.

King, David. *I Wish My Dog Would Do That.* London: Faber & Faber Ltd., 1989.

Landesman, Bill, and Kathleen Berman. *How to Train Your Dog in Six Weeks.* New York: Arco, 1984.

Monks of New Skete. *How to Be Your Dog's Best Friend: A Training Manual for Dog Owners.* Little, Brown and Co., 1978.

Neil, David H., and Clarice Rutherford. *How to Raise a Puppy You Can Live With.* Loveland, CO: Alpine Publications Inc., 1982.

Pearsall, Margaret. *The Pearsall Guide to Successful Dog Training.* 3rd ed. New York: Howell Book House, 1981.

Smith, M. L. *You Can Teach Your Dog to Eliminate on Command.* 2nd ed. Friday Harbor, WA: Smith Sager Publications, 1984.

Volhard, Joachim J., and Gail T. Fisher. *Training Your Dog: The Step-By-Step Manual.* New York: Howell Book House, 1983.

Watson, Miller. *Basic Dog Training.* Neptune City, NJ: T.F.H. Publications, Inc., 1989.

Weiss, John D. *Training a Dog to Live In Your Home: Housebreaking, Chewing, Book One.* Frankfort, IL: Animal Owners, 1980.

Wolters, Richard. *Family Dog.* Rev. ed. New York: Dutton, 1975.

Woodhouse, Barbara. *No Bad Dogs: Training Dogs the Woodhouse Way.* Simon and Schuster, 1982.

BASSET HOUNDS

Braun, Mercedes. *The New Complete Basset Hound.* 4th ed. New York: Howell Book House, 1979.

Johnston, George. *The Basset Hound.* London: Century Hutchinson Ltd., 1988.

BEAGLES

Anderson, A. C., ed. *The Beagle As an Experimental Dog.* Ames, IA: Iowa State University Press, 1970.

Berndt, Robert J. *Your Beagle.* Fairfax, VA: Denlinger's Publishers, Ltd., 1976.

Gray, Thelma. *The Beagle.* London: Century Hutchinson Ltd., 1988.

Musladin, Judith M., A. C. Musladin and Ada Lueke. *The New Beagle.* New York: Howell Book House, 1990.

Nicholas, Anna Kathterine, and Marcia Foy. *The Beagle.* Neptune City, NJ: T.F.H. Publications, Inc., 1982.

BOSTON TERRIERS

Huddleston, Arthur. *The Boston Terrier.* Fairfax, VA: Denlinger's Publishers, Ltd., 1985.

Nicholas, Anna Katherine. *The Boston Terrier.* Neptune City, NJ: T.F.H. Publications, Inc., 1988.

BOXERS

McFadden, Billie. *The New Boxer.* New York: Howell Book House, 1989.

Meyer, Lorraine C. *Your Boxer.* Fairfax, VA: Denlinger's Publishers, Ltd., 1973.

CHIHUAHUAS

Murray, Ruth L. *Your Chihuahua.* Fairfax, VA: Denlinger's Publishers, Ltd., 1966.

Nicholas, Anna Katherine. *The Chihuahua.* Neptune City, NJ: T.F.H. Publications, Inc., 1988.

Terry, Ruth E. *The New Chihuahua.* New York: Howell Book House, 1990.

CHOW CHOWS

*Atkinson, James. *Chow Chows: Everything About Puchase, Care, Nutrition, Diseases, and Training.* New York: Barron's, 1988.

**Camino E. E. & B. Co. Staff. *Chow Chow Champions 1983–1986.* Camino, CA: Camino E.E. & B. Co., 1987.

---

*Barron's publishes a series of called *The Complete Pet Owner's Manual* which includes similar books for many AKC breeds.

**Camino E.E. & B. Co. publishes similar books for many AKC breeds.

Kopatch, Kip. *The Complete Chow Chow.* New York: Howell Book House, 1988.
***Pisano, Beverly. *Chow Chows: A Complete Pet Owner's Manual.* Neptune City, NJ: T.F.H. Publications, Inc., 1990.

COCKER SPANIELS

Allen, Michael. *The American Cocker Book.* Midway City, CA: The American Cocker Magazine, 1989.
Brearley, Joan. *The Book of the Cocker Spaniel.* Neptune City, NJ: T.F.H. Publications, Inc., 1982.
Brown, Robert M. *The Cocker Spaniel Owners' Medical Manual.* Jackson, WI: Breed Manual Publications, 1987.
Grossman, Alvin. *The American Cocker Spaniel.* Wilsonville, OR: Doral Publishing, 1988.
Kane, Frank and Phyllis Wise. *A Dog Owner's Guide To American and English Cocker Spaniels.* New York: Howell Book House, 1988.
Kraeuchi, Ruth M. *The New Cocker Spaniel.* New York: Howell Book House, 1978.
Lucas-Lucas, Veronica. *The Cocker Spaniel.* London: Century Hutchinson Ltd., 1988.

COLLIES

Bishop, Ada. *All About the Collie: Rough and Smooth.* Rev. ed. London: Penguin Group, 1989.
Collie Club of America Staff. *The New Collie.* New York: Howell Book House, 1982.
Hunt, Hazel. *Rough Collies: An Owner's Companion.* New York: Howell Book House, 1990.
Osborne, Margaret. *The Collie.* London: Century Hutchinson Ltd., 1988.
Vanderlip, Sharon L. *The Collie: A Veterinay Reference for the Professional Breeder.* Cardiff by the Sea, CA: Biotechnical Veterinary Consultants, 1984.

DACHSHUNDS

Cox, Herman G. *Your Dachshund.* Fairfax, VA: Denlinger's Publishers, Ltd., 1966.
Meistrell, Lois. *The New Dachshund.* New York: Howell Book House, 1982.
Nicholas, Anna Katherine, and Marcia Foy. *The Dachshund.* Neptune City, NJ: T.F.H. Publications, Inc., 1987.

DALMATIANS

Nicholas, Anna Katherine. *The Dalmatian.* Neptune City, NJ: T.F.H. Publications, Inc., 1986.
Treen, Alfred, and Esmeralda Treen. *The Dalmatian: Coach Dog, Firehouse Dog.* New York: Howell Book House, 1980.

***T.F.H. Publications publishes a serires of KW Dog Books which includes similar books for many AKC breeds.

DOBERMAN PINSCHERS

Brown, Robert M. *The Doberman Owners' Medical Manual.* Jackson, WI: Breed Manual Publications, 1986.

Kerfman, Woodrow. *The Doberman Pinscher.* Neptune City, NJ: T.F.H. Publications, Inc., 1985.

Ladd, Mark. *Doberman: An Owner's Companion.* New York: Howell Book House 1989

Migliorini, Mario. *The Doberman Book.* New York: Arco, 1985.

Walter, Joanna and other noted authorities. *The New Doberman Pinscher.* New York: Howell Book House, 1977.

Winkler, Bernadette E. *A Beginner's Guide To Doberman Pinschers.* Neptune City, NJ: T.F.H. Publications, Inc., 1986.

ENGLISH SPRINGER SPANIELS

Goodall, Charles S., and Julia Gasow. *The New Complete English Springer Spaniel.* 3rd ed. New York: Howell Book House, 1984.

Hankwitz, Reed F. *Your English Springer Spaniel.* Fairfax, VA: Denlinger's Publishers, Ltd., 1973.

GERMAN SHEPHERD DOGS

Bennett, Jane G. *The New Complete German Shepherd Dog.* 5th ed. New York: Howell Book House, 1982.

Hart, Ernest H. *Your German Shepherd Puppy.* Rev. ed. Neptune City, NJ: T.F.H. Publications, Inc., 1987.

————. *The German Shepherd Dog.* Neptune City, NJ: T.F.H. Publications, Inc., 1984.

Ixer, Joyce. *The Alsatian (German Shepherd Dog).* Edinburgh: John Bartholomew & Son Ltd., 1985.

Lanting, Fred L. *The Total German Shepherd Dog.* Loveland, CO: Alpine Publications Inc., 1990.

Steinitz, Franklin. *A Beginner's Guide to German Shepherds.* Neptune City, NJ: T.F.H. Publications, Inc., 1987.

Strickland, Winifred and James Moses. *The German Shepherd Today—A Complete Reference for the German Shepherd Owner.* New York: Howell Book House, 1988.

GOLDEN RETRIEVERS

Donnelly, Kerry. *A Complete Introduction to Golden Retrievers.* Neptune City, NJ: T.F.H. Publications, Inc., 1987.

Fischer, Gertrude. *The New Complete Golden Retriever.* 2nd ed. New York: Howell Book House, 1984.

Sawtelle, Lucille. *All About the Golden Retriever.* New York: Penguin, 1988.

Schneider, Evelyn. *The Golden Retriever.* Fairfax, VA: Denlinger's Publishers, Ltd., 1986.

LABRADOR RETRIEVERS

Berndt, Robert J. and Richard L. Myers. *The Labrador Retriever.* Fairfax, VA: Denlinger's Publishers, Ltd., 1983.

Farrington, Selwyn Kip. *Labrador Retriever: Friend and Worker.* New York: Hastings House, 1976.

Nicholas, Anna Katherine. *A Complete Introduction to Labrador Retrievers.* Neptune City, NJ: T.F.H. Publications, Inc., 1987.

Warwick, Helen. *The Complete Labrador Retriever.* 3rd. ed. New York: Howell Book House, 1986.

Wolters, Richard. *The Labrador Retriever: The History . . . The People.* Los Angeles: Peterson Prints, 1981.

LHASA APSOS

Berndt, Robert J. *Your Lhasa Apso.* Fairfax, VA: Denlinger's Publishers, Ltd., 1982.

Herbel, Norman, and Carolyn Herbel. *The Complete Lhasa Apso.* New York: Howell Book House, 1979.

MINIATURE SCHNAUZERS

Kiedrowski, Dan. *The New Miniature Schnauzer: The Breed Since Ch. Dorem Display.* New York: Howell Book House, 1986.

Nicholas, Anna Katherine. *The Book of the Miniature Schnauzer.* Neptune City, NJ: T.F.H. Publications, Inc., 1986.

PEKINGESE

Aubrey Jones, Nigel. *The New Pekingese.* New York: Howell Book House, 1991.

Berndt, Robert J. *Your Pekingese.* Fairfax, VA: Denlinger's Publishers, Ltd., 1978.

Nicholas, Anna Katherine, and Joan McDonald Brearley. *The Book of the Pekingese.* Neptune City, NJ: T.F.H. Publications, Inc., 1990.

POMERANIANS

Hughes, Pauline B. *The Pomeranian.* Fairfax, VA: Denlinger's Publishers, Ltd., 1990.

Tietjen, Sari B. *The New Pomeranian.* New York: Howell Book House, 1987.

POODLES

Irick, Mackey J. *The New Poodle.* 6th ed. New York: Howell Book House, 1986.

Kalstone, Shirlee. *The Complete Poodle Clipping and Grooming Book.* 2nd ed. New York: Howell Book House, 1981.

LeFetra, W. *How to Clip and Groom Your Poodle.* Neptune City, NJ: T.F.H. Publications, Inc., 1969.

Meisenzahl, Hilda. *Meisen Poodle Manual.* Fairfax, VA: Denlinger's Publishers, Ltd., 1974.

Nicholas, Anna Katherine. *The Poodle.* Neptune City, NJ: T.F.H. Publications, Inc., 1984.
Sabella, Frank T. *Your Poodle: Standard, Miniature and Toy.* Fairfax, VA: Denlinger's Publishers, Ltd., 1969.

ROTTWEILERS

Freeman, Muriel. *The Complete Rottweiler.* New York: Howell Book House, 1984.
Hodinar, Dagmar. *The Rottweiler: an International Study of the Breed.* Paramus, NJ: Von Palisaden, 1986.
Nicholas, Anna Katherine. *A Complete Introduction to Rottweilers.* Neptune City, NJ: T.F.H. Publications, Inc., 1985.
Stratton, Richard F. *The Rottweiller.* Neptune City, NJ: T.F.H. Publications, Inc., 1985.
Von Beine, Heinrich. *A Step-By-Step Book About Rottweilers.* Neptune City, NJ: T.F.H. Publications, Inc., 1987.

SHETLAND SHEEPDOGS

Riddle, Maxwell. *The New Shetland Sheepdog.* New York: Howell Book House, 1974.

SHIH TZU

Brearley, Joan McDonald and Allan Easton. *The Book of The Shih Tzu.* Neptune City, NJ: T.F.H. Publications, Inc., 1980.
Easton, Allan. *This Is the Shih Tzu.* Rev. ed. Neptune City, NJ: T.F.H. Publications, Inc., 1969.
Seranne, Ann, and Lise Miller. *The Joy of Owning a Shih Tzu.* New York: Howell Book House, 1982.

SIBERIAN HUSKIES

Brearley, Joan McDonald. *This Is the Siberian Husky.* Neptune City, NJ: T.F.H. Publications, Inc., 1984.
Jennings, Michael, and Lorna B. Demidoff. *The Complete Siberian Husky.* New York: Howell Book House, 1978.
Neador, Debbie. *Siberian Huskies: The Family Album.* Fairfax, VA: Denlinger's Publishers, Ltd., 1985.

YORKSHIRE TERRIERS

Brearley, Joan McDonald. *The Book of The Yorkshire Terrier.* Neptune City, NJ: T.F.H. Publications, Inc., 1984.
Gordon, Joan, and Janet Bennett. *The Complete Yorkshire Terrier.* New York: Howell Book House, 1976.
Howard, Morris. *Your Yorkshire Terrier.* 2nd ed. Farfax, VA: Denlinger's Publishers, Ltd., 1979.